守護霊インタビュー

ドナルド・トランプ

アメリカ復活への戦略

大川隆法
Ryuho Okawa

Preface

We, Japanese, are looking for a strong America.

Here, we've found a strong new U.S. president-to-be through "Spiritual Interview with the Guardian Spirit of Donald Trump".

I hope he (Mr. Donald Trump) will be a great new leader of the U.S. And, I, myself, want to believe his honesty, bravery, and friendship.

We expect him to succeed in diplomacy and economic policy.

May God save America and the world!

January 11, 2016
Master & CEO of Happy Science Group
Ryuho Okawa

(和訳）序文

　私たち日本人は、強いアメリカを求めている。

　なんとこの本で、私たちは、強い次期大統領候補を見つけたのだ。それがこの『ドナルド・トランプ氏の守護霊へのスピリチュアル・インタビュー』だ。

　私も、彼（ドナルド・トランプ氏）が偉大なる次期アメリカ合衆国のリーダーの器(うつわ)であることを望んでいる。

　そして、私自身、彼の正直さ、勇気、友情に期待を寄せている。

　彼が外交と経済政策で成功されんことを。

　神よ、アメリカと世界を救いたまえ！

2016年1月11日

幸福(こうふく)の科学(かがく)グループ創始者兼総裁(そうししゃけんそうさい)

大川隆法(おおかわりゅうほう)

Contents

Preface 2

1 The Guardian Spirit of "The Next President"
    Trump Appears 14
    I'm Trump, but not a *candidate* 18

2 The True Intention in the Violent Remarks Against
    Immigrants 22
    I, myself, am advertising 22
    Japan should be the one to open up and accept
    immigrants 30

3 On the Criticisms from the Mass Media 36
    Criticism is a New York cheesecake 40

4 Honesty Shows as Discrimination against Women 46
    I'm giving meat to hungry lions 50

5 Views On Japan-U.S. Ties, Japan-South Korea Ties,
    Russia, Iran and China 54
    Japan should shut up if it cannot protect itself 54
    South Korea must have a respectful attitude toward Japan 58

目　次

(和訳) 序文 ……………………………………………………… 3

1 「次期大統領」トランプ守護霊登場 ……………………… 15

　「私はトランプだが、大統領『候補』じゃない」 ……… 19

2 移民に関する過激な発言の真意は ……………………… 23

　私自身が「広告そのもの」 …………………………………… 23
　日本こそ「開国」して移民を受け入れるべき …………… 31

3 メディアからの批判をどう思っているか ……………… 37
　批判は「ニューヨークチーズケーキ」 …………………… 41

4 女性差別と言われるのは「素直だから」 ……………… 47
　「飢えたライオン」に肉を与えている ……………………… 51

5 日米、日韓、ロシア、イラン、中国をどう見るか … 55

　「日本は自分で守れないなら黙るべき」 ………………… 55
　韓国には日本を尊敬する姿勢が必要 ……………………… 59

	If I were Putin, I would do something this year 62
	China's plan is complicating things in the Middle East 66
6	What Would Hillary Bring As the President? 70
7	Recovering the U.S. Economy 76
	I'm an economist who receives inspiration from Heaven 76
	The new force regarding business 82
	I believe in God 88
8	Expectations for the Muslim Immigrants in the U.S. 92
9	Form a Triangle of God-Believing Countries and Stand Against Atheist China 100
	The successful method for Japan 100
	Protect against the next Hitler by forming a U.S.-Japan-Germany triangle 104
10	Trump's Past Lives and a "Big Name" 110
11	Message for the Prosperity of Japan and the U.S. 120
	After the spiritual interview 126

★ This spiritual interview was given in English. The Japanese text is a translation by the Happy Science International Editorial Division.

「もし私がプーチンなら、今年、何かをやる」 63
　　　中東情勢を難しくしている中国の動き 67
6　もしヒラリーが大統領になったら？ 71
7　アメリカ経済回復のための考え方 77
　　　天からインスピレーションを受ける
　　　「経済の専門家」 77
　　　ビジネスのための新たな「フォース」(力) 83
　　　「私は神を信じている」 89
8　米国内のムスリム移民に望むこと 93
9　「神を信じる」トライアングルで無神論の中国に
　　対抗せよ 101
　　　日本にとっての「成功の道」とは 101
　　　米・日・独の三国で「次なるヒットラー」に対する
　　　守りを 105
10　過去世を問われて飛び出したビッグ・ネーム 111
11　日米の繁栄に向けたメッセージ 121
　　　霊言を終えて 127

※本書は、英語で収録された霊言に和訳を付けたものです。

This book is the transcript of spiritual messages given by the guardian spirit of Donald Trump.

These spiritual messages were channeled through Ryuho Okawa. However, please note that because of his high level of enlightenment, his way of receiving spiritual messages is fundamentally different from other psychic mediums who undergo trances and are completely taken over by the spirits they are channeling.

Each human soul is made up of six soul siblings, one of whom acts as the guardian spirit of the person living on earth. People living on earth are connected to their guardian spirits at the innermost subconscious level. They are a part of people's very souls and therefore, exact reflections of their thoughts and philosophies.

It should be noted that these spiritual messages are opinions of the individual spirits and may contradict the ideas or teachings of the Happy Science Group.

本書は、ドナルド・トランプの守護霊霊言を収録したものである。

　「霊言現象」とは、あの世の霊存在の言葉を語り下ろす現象のことをいう。これは高度な悟りを開いた者に特有のものであり、「霊媒現象」（トランス状態になって意識を失い、霊が一方的にしゃべる現象）とは異なる。

　また、人間の魂は６人のグループからなり、あの世に残っている「魂の兄弟」の１人が守護霊を務めている。つまり、守護霊は、実は自分自身の魂の一部である。

　したがって、「守護霊の霊言」とは、いわば、本人の潜在意識にアクセスしたものであり、その内容は、その人が潜在意識で考えていること（本心）と考えてよい。

　ただ、「霊言」は、あくまでも霊人の意見であり、幸福の科学グループとしての見解と矛盾する内容を含む場合がある点、付記しておきたい。

Spiritual Interview with the Guardian Spirit of Donald Trump

January 5, 2016 at Happy Science General Headquarters, Tokyo

守護霊インタビュー
ドナルド・トランプ
アメリカ復活への戦略

2016年1月5日　東京都・幸福の科学総合本部にて

Donald Trump (1946 – Present)

A candidate running for the 2016 U.S. presidential election [Republican]. An American entrepreneur and TV personality. Chairman and president of the Trump Organization.

Born in New York City. After graduating from the University of Pennsylvania in 1968, he began to work at his father's real estate company and was given control of the company in 1971. Caught the media's attention upon completing the Trump Tower on Fifth Avenue in New York in 1983, a building some people call to be the most expensive in the world. Trump is known as a real estate magnate, making millions and billions due to his great success in real estate development and hotel and casino management. His autobiography published when he was 41 years old became a bestseller. Trump has works on success theory and has been making many appearances in the media.

Trump made his presidential announcement in June 2015 and has been gaining support from many groups of people as the lead Republican candidate.

Interviewers from Happy Science

Yuki Oikawa

> Director of Foreign Affairs
> Happiness Realization Party

Masashi Ishikawa

> Director General of International Editorial Division

Mariko Isis

> Vice Chairperson of the Board of Directors
> Supervisor of International Headquarters

※ Interviewers are listed in the order that they appear in the transcript.
The professional titles represent the position at the time of the interview.

ドナルド・トランプ（1946 ー）

　2016年アメリカ合衆国大統領選挙候補者（共和党）。アメリカの実業家、テレビパーソナリティ。不動産会社「トランプ・オーガナイゼーション」会長。

　ニューヨーク市生まれ。1968年ペンシルベニア大学卒業後、不動産業を営む父親の会社に入り、71年、経営権を与えられる。83年、「世界一豪華なビル」トランプ・タワーをニューヨーク五番街に建て、全米の話題を呼ぶ。不動産開発やホテル、カジノ経営などで大成功を収め、巨万の富を築き、「不動産王」と呼ばれる。41歳のとき出版した自伝はベストセラーになり、成功論に関する著作やメディア露出も多い。

　2015年6月、2016年アメリカ合衆国大統領選挙出馬を発表。以降、継続してトップの支持率を保っている。

質問者（幸福の科学）

及川幸久（幸福実現党外務局長）

石川雅士（国際編集局長）

イシス真理子（幸福の科学副理事長 兼 国際本部担当）

※質問順。役職は収録当時のもの。

1 The Guardian Spirit of "The Next President" Trump Appears

Ryuho Okawa I'll invite the guardian spirit of Mr. Donald Trump, the famous candidate running for the U.S. presidency. He's a very difficult person, I guess. He has a lot of techniques to get the heart of the people, so you must be careful and watchful. Please see through his real mind from your accurate questions.

I guess he, himself, intends to make this a big chance for himself to get Japanese support for his presidency, so be careful with your questions.

This is his autobiography, "A Man Who Will Change America - Donald Trump" [English translation of the Japanese title of *Trump: The Art of the Deal*]. It was originally published in 1987 and its translation was sold in Japan the next year, in 1988. At the time, he was a very handsome person at only 42 and already

1 「次期大統領」トランプ守護霊登場

大川隆法　アメリカ大統領選に出馬(しゅつば)を表明している有名な候補者である、ドナルド・トランプ氏の守護霊をお招きしたいと思います。なかなか難しい人物かと思われます。人の心を掴(つか)むテクニックをいろいろと持っている方ですので、気をつけないといけません。ぜひ、的(まと)を射(い)た質問で、本心を見抜いてください。

　たぶん、ご本人は、この機会に日本人からも大統領選について支持を得たいと思っていると思われますので、質問には、注意してください。

　（本を見せながら）これは『トランプ自伝―アメリカを変える男』という彼の自伝です。もとの本は1987年にアメリカで出て、翌1988年に日本で翻訳が出ました。当時、彼は

『トランプ自伝―アメリカを変える男』
(1988年 ドナルド・J・トランプ、トニー・シュウォーツ共著、枝松真一訳、早川書房)

had 400 billion yen. He was very handsome at that time. Now, I don't know [laughs], but he used to be.

Today's aim is to get his real thinking and real attitude, for example, on international politics, Japan, Japanese people, Okinawa, China, Russia and Islamic people. We must learn from his guardian spirit what he really believes.

OK? Then, we will start, but he's a bit difficult, so be careful. Please be strong. OK? [Claps hands three times.] Then, I'll invite him. [Claps hands once.]

The guardian spirit of Mr. Donald Trump, would you come down here? We want to ask you several questions. Mr. Donald Trump, the candidate for the U.S. presidency, Donald Trump, would you come down here? This is Happy Science General Headquarters in Tokyo.

[Summons his guardian spirit]
[About 10 seconds of silence]

まだ42歳で、非常にスマートで、すでに4000億円も資産がありました。当時は非常にスマートですね。今はどうか分かりませんが（笑）、当時はスマートでした。

　今日は、国際政治であるとか、日本や日本人、沖縄、中国、ロシア、イスラムの人々などに関しての「彼の考え方」「本音」を知るのが狙いです。彼の守護霊から、本音を聞き出さないといけません。

　よろしいですか。では始めますが、やや難しい人ですので注意してください。負けないでください。よろしいですか（手を三回叩く）。では招霊します（手を一回叩く）。

　ドナルド・トランプ氏の守護霊よ、どうかこちらにお越しください。いくつか質問させていただきたく思います。合衆国の大統領候補であるドナルド・トランプ氏よ、ドナルド・トランプよ、こちらにお越しください。ここは東京にある幸福の科学総合本部です。

（招霊する）
（約10秒間の沈黙）

I'm Trump, but not a *candidate*

Trump's G.S. Hmm…

Yuki Oikawa Mr. Trump?

Trump's G.S. Oh?

Oikawa Thank you for…

Trump's G.S. Oh, you speak English. OK, OK. Not so bad. Hmm.

Oikawa Thank you very much for joining us today. Do you realize that you were invited to Happy Science General Headquarters in Japan?

Trump's G.S. Huh? Huh? What?

「私はトランプだが、大統領『候補』じゃない」

トランプ守護霊　うーん……。

及川幸久　トランプ氏でしょうか。

トランプ守護霊　うん?

及川　ありがとうござい……。

トランプ守護霊　ああ、英語が話せるのか。そうか、そうか。悪くないね。うん。

及川　本日は、お越しくださり、まことにありがとうございます。日本の幸福の科学総合本部に招かれたということは、お分かりでしょうか。

トランプ守護霊　うん?　何?　何だって?

1 The Guardian Spirit of "The Next President" Trump Appears

Oikawa Do you realize that you were invited to Happy Science General Headquarters?

Trump's G.S. What do you mean by "realize"?

Oikawa Are you aware of where you are?

Trump's G.S. You just called me, so I came here. I'm Donald Trump, but I'm not a *candidate* for the presidency. I'm the *next president*, you know? Please call me, "The Next President, Mr. Trump." It's the formal standard. OK?

Oikawa Yes, OK. This is your opportunity to have your spiritual interview through Master Ryuho Okawa here. You can just relax, because we are not attacking you. We are not CNN or NBC.

Trump's G.S. Really? Sneak attack, I can guess.

及川　幸福の科学の総合本部に招かれたことは、お分かりでしょうか。

トランプ守護霊　「分かる」とは、どういう意味かね。

及川　ここがどこか、お分かりでしょうか。

トランプ守護霊　呼ばれたから来たんじゃないか。私はドナルド・トランプだが、大統領「候補」じゃないよ。「次期大統領」だからね。「次期大統領、ドナルド・トランプ氏」と呼んでくれたまえ。それが正式な呼び方だから。いいね？

及川　はい、分かりました。今日は、こちらの大川隆法総裁を通じての霊言の機会となります。どうか、リラックスなさってください。あなたを攻撃するつもりはありません。ＣＮＮやＮＢＣではありませんので。

トランプ守護霊　本当かい？　「スニーク・アタック（「卑怯な攻撃」の意。太平洋戦争の日本軍による真珠湾攻撃を

Oikawa We are not that kind of people.

Trump's G.S. Oh, really?

2 The True Intention in the Violent Remarks Against Immigrants

I, myself, am advertising

Oikawa Now, we would like to ask you several questions, OK?

Trump's G.S. OK. Are you a good man?

Oikawa Yes, I am. We all are. Thank you, Mr. Trump. Here's the first question. You were divisive force in U.S. politics last year by a succession of discriminatory remarks against Mexicans, women and Muslims.

意味することが多い)」しようと思っても分かるからね。

及川　そんなことはしませんので。

トランプ守護霊　本当かい？

2　移民に関する過激な発言の真意は

私自身が「広告そのもの」

及川　では、いくつか質問してもよろしいでしょうか。

トランプ守護霊　ああ。君はいい人なのかな。

及川　もちろん、全員そうです。ありがとうございます。最初の質問です。あなたは昨年、メキシコ人や、女性、イスラム教徒に対する、一連の差別的な（discriminatory）発言で、アメリカの政治の分裂を進める勢力でした。

Trump's G.S. You are an enemy [audience laugh].

Oikawa OK. However. However, you faced many criticisms and you got a huge media coverage. Even so, your rating is still very high and you are a frontrunner.

Trump's G.S. Frontrunner? No, next president [audience laugh].

2 移民に関する過激な発言の真意は

トランプ守護霊　やっぱり〝敵〟だな（会場笑）。

及川　分かりました。しかしです。しかし、多くの批判に直面し、メディアが大々的に報道したにもかかわらず、あなたの支持率は今なお非常に高く、フロント・ランナーです。

トランプ守護霊　フロント・ランナー？　いや、次期大統領だ（会場笑）。

(Left) Trump giving a speech during a rally in Mississippi, January 2, 2016. In his presidential announcement in June 2015, he stated that Mexicans "are bringing drugs, are bringing crime and are rapists." Despite making many controversial statements, Trump remains the frontrunner of Republican candidates. After the California shooting incident in December, he called for a ban on Muslims entering the United States. Even so, the CNN/ORC poll later that month showed Trump leading the Republican race at a whopping 39% and Senator Ted Cruz in second place at 18%.

No political analyst could foresee that, out of the 12 Republican presidential candidates [as of December 30], Trump will maintain the lead through the New Year. His high approval rating may be coming from his candid statements that represent the voices of Republican voters.

2016年1月2日、ミシシッピ州における集会で演説するトランプ（左写真）。2015年6月の大統領選出馬表明演説で、いきなり、メキシコ人は「麻薬や犯罪を持ちこむ強姦魔だ」と発言。以来、さまざまな「問題発言」を繰り返しているにもかかわらず、共和党の指名候補争いでトップの支持率を保ち続けている。12月にはカリフォルニアでの銃乱射テロ事件を受け、「イスラム教徒入国禁止」発言をしたが、同下旬に発表されたＣＮＮ／ＯＲＣの世論調査では全米の39％の支持率を獲得し、18％で2位のテッド・クルーズ上院議員に大差をつけた。

共和党の大統領候補12人（12月30日現在）中、トランプが支持率首位のまま年を越すとは、専門家らは誰も予想しなかった。歯に衣着せぬ発言で共和党支持者の思いを代弁していることが、高支持率の理由と見られる。

Oikawa OK. Did your success so far and people's reactions to your blunt attitude and style surprise you or not?

Trump's G.S. Hmm… What's the problem? I can't understand. I'm very popular in the United States. You, the Japanese, don't know my real popularity. So, I can't understand your first question. Criminality?

Oikawa Discrimination.

Trump's G.S. Discrimination?! Oh, no, no, no. I'm a person of love for the world! You misunderstood me already. I just said on behalf of a small portion of people of the United States; people who hate such kind of illegal people living in the United States that insist a lot of rights without paying taxes. I just represented such an opinion through my mouth, so it's not my real idea. I just checked it.

及川　はい。ここまでの成功や、あなたのそっけない態度、あなたのスタイルに対する人々の反応は、意外ですか、それとも、そんなことはありませんか。

トランプ守護霊　うーん……。何が問題なわけ？　分からんね。私はアメリカで大人気なんだから。君たち日本人は、私の本当の人気を知らないんだよ。だから、君の最初の質問……「犯罪性」(criminality) だったかな？

及川　「差別」です。

トランプ守護霊　差別⁉　違う、違う、違う。私は世界に対する愛に溢れた人間なんだから！　もう誤解してるじゃないか。私は単に、ごく一部の米国民の意見を口にしたにすぎない。アメリカに住んでいて、「権利ばかり主張して、税金は納めない、違法な連中」なんかを嫌っている国民の意見を、この口を通して代弁しただけにすぎない。だから、私の本心じゃないよ。チェックしただけだから。

Oikawa Master Ryuho Okawa talked about your technique before this interview. Are you using any other advertising techniques in your campaign?

Trump's G.S. Oh, no, no, no. I, myself, am advertising, so I don't need any advertising. I, myself, am advertising. I am the Trump Tower itself. I, myself, am very famous. So, I don't need any technique.

Oikawa You are always honest? Is that what you mean?

及川　大川隆法総裁は、このインタビューの前に、あなたのテクニックについて話されたのですが、選挙運動のなかで、何か他の広告テクニックは使っていますか。

トランプ守護霊　いや、いや、いや。私自身が「広告そのもの」だから、広告なんて、まったく必要ない。私自身が広告であり、私が「トランプ・タワーそのもの」なんだから。私自身がすごく有名なので、テクニックなんか必要ない。

及川　常に正直であるということですか。

(Left) The 68-story, 202-m [663-ft] Trump Tower on Fifth Avenue in New York. Opened in 1983. The upper floors are occupied as first-class residential areas. The tower is the symbol of Donald Trump, a real estate tycoon from New York City.
　ニューヨーク5番街にある、高さ202メートル68階建てのトランプ・タワー（左写真）。1983年オープン。高層階は超高級住宅になっており、ニューヨーク市出身の不動産王ドナルド・トランプのシンボルである。

Trump's G.S. Oh, yeah, yeah. Honesty is my best virtue, I think. Honesty is the best. Honesty is the best way to get money and succeed in business.

Japan should be the one to open up and accept immigrants

Oikawa More recently, you have said you would stop immigration for those of the Muslim faith and deport many Muslims from your country. Is that what you are planning to do when you become the president?

Trump's G.S. It's a great task of the American president. Islamic immigrants are a very important matter. I'm honest, so I fought this matter. It's not good in terms of populism, but I'm honest.

I'm not Hitler. I'm quite opposite to Hitler. So I, myself, warned against them. If they all come to the United States in my presidency, they will suffer a lot of problems. I already warned them. So, I'm not Hitler.

トランプ守護霊 ああ、はい、はい。正直が、私の最大の美徳だと思ってるけどね。正直が一番です。お金を儲けてビジネスで成功するには、正直が一番。

日本こそ「開国」して移民を受け入れるべき

及川 あなたは最近、ムスリムの移民について言及されましたね。イスラム教の信仰を持つ移民は入国できないようにし、アメリカ国内からムスリムを排斥すると言われました。大統領になったら、それをやろうと考えているわけでしょうか。

トランプ守護霊 それはアメリカ大統領の大きな仕事だからな。イスラムの移民は非常に重要な問題だ。私は正直だから、この問題と戦った。ポピュリズムからすれば、まずいんだが、私は正直だからね。

　私はヒットラーじゃない。ヒットラーとは正反対だ。だから、自ら彼らに警告した。もし彼らが全部、私の大統領任期中にアメリカに来たら、多くの問題に苦しむことになると。すでに警告したわけだ。だから、ヒットラーとは違

I am more conscientious. I have more conscience regarding immigrants.

But immigration is a deep, deep problem in the U.S., so you, the Japanese, don't know about that. You already keep a closed-door policy in Japan, so you have no right to criticize me about that!

Oikawa Do you have any suggestions to the Japanese people or government?

Trump's G.S. Open! Open your country. Open your country.

Oikawa Accept more people from other countries?

Trump's G.S. Yeah! It's your obligation. Please accept all the immigrants who are suffering from the war of the Islamic matter. You must accept the Syrian people and the people who are living in Iraq and the Islamic State. You are responsible for that. I think so.

う。私のほうが良心的だよ。移民に関して良心的なんだ。

　だが、移民問題はアメリカにとって実に根が深くて、君たち日本人には分からんだろう。日本はもう〝鎖国政策〟を守ってるんだから、私のことをとやかく言う権利はないね！

及川　日本人や日本政府に対して、何か提案はありますか。

トランプ守護霊　開けなさい！　開国だよ。開国しなさい。

及川　もっと他の国から人を受け入れろと。

トランプ守護霊　そう！　それが義務です。イスラム関係の戦争で苦しんでいる移民を全員、受け入れてください。シリアの人もイラクに住んでいる人も、イスラム国の人も、受け入れないといけません。そうする責任があると思いますがね。

Masashi Ishikawa Excuse me.

Trump's G.S. OK!

Ishikawa So, you mean the Japanese population is decreasing and that's why we need to accept immigrants?

Trump's G.S. OK. OK.

Ishikawa But the American population is increasing, so you don't have to accept immigrants? Do you mean it like that? No? Is it our responsibility?

Trump's G.S. Hmm… I don't know your problem of a decreasing population, but you have money for such kind of poor and miserable people. If you have a lot of mercy, please accept these people. In America, we are already suffering from a lot of discrimination. We have been struggling. But you've never experienced such kind of problem. So, if you are the top runner of

石川雅士　失礼します。

トランプ守護霊　どうぞ！

石川　つまり、日本の人口が減っているので移民を受け入れる必要があるということでしょうか。

トランプ守護霊　はい、はい。

石川　しかし、アメリカは人口が増えているので、移民は受け入れなくていいと、そうおっしゃりたいのでしょうか。違いますか。私たちの責任なのでしょうか。

トランプ守護霊　うーん……。おたくの国の人口減少の問題については分からんが、そういう貧しくて悲惨な人たちを救うための金はあるだろう。慈悲の心が篤いなら、その人たちを受け入れてくださいよ。アメリカは、すでにいろいろな差別問題で苦しんでいる。ずっと戦ってきたんだよ。だが、君たちは一度も経験したことがない。だから、世界の国々のトップランナーなら、そうした問題を経験しない

the countries worldwide, you must experience such a problem. It will be your test as the leader of the world.

Ishikawa So, America is a great nation…

Trump's G.S. Yeah. Indeed.

Ishikawa …that has accepted many immigrants so far.

Trump's G.S. America has Donald Trump. This is the certification of a great country. [Laughs.]

3 On the Criticisms from the Mass Media

Ishikawa I heard that your campaign slogan is, "Make America Great Again."

Trump's G.S. Oh, yeah, yeah, yeah.

といかん。それが世界のリーダーとしてのテストだろう。

石川　つまり、アメリカは偉大な国で……。

トランプ守護霊　そう。その通り。

石川　今までたくさんの移民を受け入れてきたと。

トランプ守護霊　アメリカに、ドナルド・トランプあり。それが、偉大な国であることの証明書だ。ハハハハハ。

3　メディアからの批判をどう思っているか

石川　あなたの選挙戦のスローガンは「アメリカを再び偉大な国に」だそうですが。

トランプ守護霊　ああ、そう、そう、そう。

3 On the Criticisms from the Mass Media

Ishikawa This slogan is the same as that of Ronald Reagan, I think…

Trump's G.S. Ronald Reagan? I hate him. I hate him.

Ishikawa Really? I thought you respected him… Do you really hate him?

Trump's G.S. He is poor in mind. In reality, he had some problem in his head during his presidency. He was an actor, so he played as the president, but he was not a real president.

Ishikawa Oh, really? I thought he was a great hero in the Republican Party.

Trump's G.S. No, no, no, no, no, no, no. He pretended to be a great leader of the Republicans. I have real power, real knowledge, real activity and real

石川　このスローガンはロナルド・レーガンのものと同じだと思うのですが……。

トランプ守護霊　ロナルド・レーガンか。私は嫌いだね。嫌いだ。

石川　本当ですか。尊敬されているのかと……。本当に嫌いなんですか。

トランプ守護霊　彼は心が貧しい。実際、大統領の任期中から脳に何か問題があったんだ。彼は俳優だったから、俳優みたいに大統領の役を演じたけれど、本物の大統領じゃなかったね。

石川　そうですか？　共和党の偉大なヒーローだと思っていました。

トランプ守護霊　違う。違う。違う。違う。違う。違う。違う。共和党の偉大なヒーローのふりをしていたんだ。私こそ、アメリカ大統領になれるだけの本物の力、本物の知

capability to become an American president. The first and the last president of America.

Criticism is a New York cheesecake

Ishikawa This is Mr. Yuta's request. He is Master Okawa's son. The mass media always exaggerate your comments badly and as a result, you are criticized a lot. Maybe you don't mind these criticisms, but what do you think about their mindset? Is it evil or…

Trump's G.S. It's just because I'm strong. That's the reason. I'm strong. Hmm.

Ishikawa So, no problem, then?

Trump's G.S. No problem. I'm strong.

識、本物の活動、本物の能力がある。最初にして最後のアメリカ大統領だ。

批判は「ニューヨークチーズケーキ」

石川　これは裕太さんからの質問です。大川総裁のご子息です。マスメディアは、常にあなたの発言を悪い方向に誇張し、その結果として、あなたは批判されてばかりですよね。そういった批判は気にしていらっしゃらないのかもしれませんが、マスメディアのものの考え方について、どう思われますか。悪であるとか、あるいは……。

トランプ守護霊　「私が強いから」というだけのことだよ。理由はそこだ。私は強い。うん。

石川　では、「問題ない」と。

トランプ守護霊　問題ない。強いから。

3 On the Criticisms from the Mass Media

Oikawa So, you are not afraid of criticisms from the mass media?

Trump's G.S. I'm not afraid of any criticisms. I am the strongest president. Hmm. I think so.

Ishikawa But you said...

Trump's G.S. I already am the president.

Ishikawa So, you are special, then.

Trump's G.S. Obama, "the black angel from Hell," is already dead.

Oikawa Maybe the other politicians in the U.S. are afraid of criticisms by the press.

Trump's G.S. Oh, really?

3　メディアからの批判をどう思っているか

及川　マスメディアからの批判など怖くないということですね。

トランプ守護霊　どんな批判も怖くない。私こそ最強の大統領だ。うん。そう思っとる。

石川　しかし、あなたは……。

トランプ守護霊　もう、すでに大統領だから。

石川　あなたは特別だと。

トランプ守護霊　〝地獄の黒天使〟オバマは、すでに死んでいる。

及川　アメリカの他の政治家は、メディアの批判を恐れているのかもしれません。

トランプ守護霊　ほう、そうかい。

3 On the Criticisms from the Mass Media

Oikawa But you are so tough. How?

Trump's G.S. Because…

Oikawa Are you using the power of the press?

Trump's G.S. Criticism is my favorite. It's a sweet dessert for me. When you want a cup of coffee, you want some cake or something like that, right? For me, criticism is a New York cheesecake.

Ishikawa I think you said politicians should be cautious about dealing with the mass media. But you are special, you are different. Ordinary politicians should be cautious.

Trump's G.S. For me, criticism is an advertisement in disguise. Every criticism will be advertising for me because I'm strong. I'm confident of my ability!

及川　それなのに、あなたはなぜ、そんなにタフでいられるのですか。

トランプ守護霊　それは……。

及川　報道の力を利用しているのですか。

トランプ守護霊　批判は〝大好物〟だからさ。甘いデザートだな。コーヒーが飲みたくなったときは、ケーキとかそういうものが食べたくなるだろう。私にしてみれば、批判は、ニューヨークチーズケーキだな。

石川　あなたは「政治家はマスメディアの対応に気を付けるべきだ」とおっしゃったと思います。しかし、あなたは特別で、違うわけですね。普通の政治家は気を付けるべきなのだと。

トランプ守護霊　批判は私から見れば、姿を変えた広告なんだよ。どんな批判も私の宣伝になる。私が強いからだ。能力に関しては自信がある！

4 Honesty Shows as Discrimination against Women

Mariko Isis Yes. I can feel that from you, as I see you on TV.

Trump's G.S. Ah, a beautiful lady.

Isis Thank you so much. You're looking nice, too.

Trump's G.S. Why are you sitting there? You're young, beautiful and clever.

Isis [Laughs.] Thank you so much. Many people criticize you…

Trump's G.S. Oh? Really? I don't know. I don't know.

Isis … saying that you are discriminating against

4　女性差別と言われるのは「素直だから」

イシス真理子　そうですね。私も、テレビであなたを見ていて、それを感じます。

トランプ守護霊　おお、美しいレディーですね。

イシス　ありがとうございます。あなたも素敵ですよ。

トランプ守護霊　どうして、そんなところに座ってるの。若くて美しくて賢いのに。

イシス　（笑）ありがとうございます。あなたは多くの人から批判されていますよね……。

トランプ守護霊　え、本当？　知りません。知りませんよ。

イシス　「女性を差別している」と。でも、いろいろなテ

women. But as I see you in a lot of TV programs, I feel that you're just an honest man.

Trump's G.S. Honest man. Yeah, yeah. That's right.

Isis You're just honest, too honest.

Trump's G.S. Too honest!

Isis If you think that a woman doesn't look good, you just say it, right?

Trump's G.S. [Taps on the cover of his autobiography with his portrait on it.]

[Audience laugh.]

Trump's G.S. Nice young man. Used to be.

Isis Yes, you do look good. Well, I wanted to ask you,

4 女性差別と言われるのは「素直だから」

レビであなたを観ていると、正直者だというだけのような気がします。

トランプ守護霊　正直者。そうそう、まさにその通り。

イシス　あなたは正直なだけ、正直すぎるだけなんですよね。

トランプ守護霊　正直すぎるか！

イシス　だから、女性の見た目がよくないと思ったら、そのまま言ってしまうんですよね。

トランプ守護霊　（自伝を取り上げ、表紙に出ている自分の写真を何度も叩いてみせる）

（会場笑）

トランプ守護霊　若くて、いい男だったんだよ。

イシス　はい、カッコいいと思います。それで、お聞きし

do you intend to do that or does your mouth just slip? Are you just honest? Or, are you using the mass media to be rude? Are you intending to be rude?

Trump's G.S. OK, OK, OK, OK, OK, OK.

Isis Most people think that you're rude. But I just think you're honest.

I'm giving meat to hungry lions

Trump's G.S. I appreciate your friendship very much. I appreciate you, but the mass media have their business. They need a lot of articles to write, so they want articles every day. They are hungry. They are hungry lions, I mean. The reality of the mass media is that they are hungry lions. Hungry lions need meat. A lot of raw meat. So, I, myself, want to give them meat.

たいのですが、意図的にそうしているのでしょうか、もしくは、単に口が滑ってしまうのでしょうか。正直なだけで。それとも、マスメディアを使って無礼に見せているとか。わざと無礼にしているのですか。

トランプ守護霊　オーケー、オーケー、オーケー、分かった、分かった、分かった。

イシス　あなたは、ほとんどの人から無礼だと思われています。でも私は、正直なだけだと思います。

「飢えたライオン」に肉を与えている

トランプ守護霊　あなたの友情には深く感謝しますよ。感謝はするけど、マスメディアだって商売だからね。記事をたくさん書く必要があって、毎日欲しがってる。腹をすかせている。要は、飢えたライオンだ。マスメディアの実態は、「飢えたライオン」なんだよ。飢えたライオンは肉が欲しい。生肉がたくさん。だから、肉を与えてやりたくなる。

4 Honesty Shows as Discrimination against Women

Isis So, you're doing an act of love.

Trump's G.S. To give.

Isis To give them more meat.

Trump's G.S. Yeah. So, they can write about me, earn money and make a living. It's my love for them. I love the mass media very much.

Isis Yes, and as a result of that, you are loved much more by men than women because you are just honest. But I think that is the reason why you are popular.

4　女性差別と言われるのは「素直だから」

イシス　では、愛を実践しているわけですね。

トランプ守護霊　与えてやる。

イシス　彼らにもっと肉を与えると。

トランプ守護霊　そう。だからメディアは私について書くことができて、お金も稼げて、生活していくことができる。つまり、彼らに対する私の愛なんだよ。マスメディアは大好きだから。

イシス　ええ、その結果として、女性より男性のほうがずっとあなたを好きなんですよね。あなたは本当に正直なので。でも、そこが、あなたの人気の理由だと思います。

5 Views On Japan-U.S. Ties, Japan-South Korea Ties, Russia, Iran and China

Japan should shut up if it cannot protect itself

Isis And I wanted to ask you another question about the U.S.-Japan Security Treaty.

Trump's G.S. Security Treaty?

Isis Yes. You said that it is unfair…

Trump's G.S. Unfair, unfair. Unfair is a good…

Isis … for the United States to have to go and save Japan when Japan is in danger, but the Japanese people don't have to save Americans.

5　日米、日韓、ロシア、イラン、中国をどう見るか

「日本は自分で守れないなら黙るべき」

イシス　それから、日米安保条約についても質問したかったのですが。

トランプ守護霊　安保条約？

イシス　はい。あなたは「不公平」だと……。

トランプ守護霊　不公平、不公平ね。不公平というのは、いい……。

イシス　アメリカは、日本が危ないときは日本を助けに来なければいけないのに、日本はアメリカを助けなくてもいいので。

Trump's G.S. I hate the Okinawan people. We, the American army, are protecting Japan from the enemies of Japan, but they hate us, do a lot of demonstrations and say, "Yankee, go home." And there is the Henoko problem in Okinawa. If they want to do so, please protect it by yourselves. Please have nuclear weapons in Japan. If you cannot do that, then shut up, Japanese! Shut up, Okinawa!

Isis So, if you become the president, you are going to say that?

Trump's G.S. I'm already the president.

Isis Yes, OK.

Trump's G.S. Virtually. In the supernatural world.

5　日米、日韓、ロシア、イラン、中国をどう見るか

トランプ守護霊　沖縄の人たちは好かんね。われわれ米軍が日本を敵から守ってやってるのに、彼らはわれわれを憎んで、デモばかりやって、「ヤンキー、ゴーホーム」と言ってる。沖縄には辺野古問題もあるし。そうしたいんなら、どうぞ自分たちで守ってください。どうぞ日本も核兵器を持ってください。それができないんなら、日本人は黙ってなさい！　沖縄は黙ってなさい！

イシス　では、あなたが大統領になったら、それを言うつもりなんですね。

トランプ守護霊　私はすでに大統領だよ。

イシス　そうですね、はい。

トランプ守護霊　事実上はね。〝超自然の世界〟では。

South Korea must have a respectful attitude toward Japan

Isis OK. And as South Korea is near Japan, what do you think about South Korea? Last year, South Korea and Japan reached an agreement on the comfort women issue*.

Trump's G.S. Ah, comfort women issue. No, no.

Isis Can you tell us what you think of Japan and South Korea?

Trump's G.S. I don't know the reality, but it's not recommendable for the dignity of the Korean people. It's rude. It will make many difficulties between South Korea and Japan.

South Korea has a very difficult emotion about Japan,

---

* On December 28, 2015, the Japanese and South Korean governments agreed to "a final and irreversible" resolution regarding the comfort women issue.

5　日米、日韓、ロシア、イラン、中国をどう見るか

韓国には日本を尊敬する姿勢が必要

イシス　はい。そして、韓国は日本と近いのですが、韓国についてはどう思われますか。去年、韓国と日本は慰安婦問題について合意に達しました（注）。

トランプ守護霊　ああ、慰安婦問題か。駄目だねえ。

イシス　日本と韓国についてはどう思われるか、お話しいただけますか。

トランプ守護霊　事実に関しては知らないけど、韓国人の尊厳を考えると、お勧めできないね。無礼だよ。日韓の間に多くの困難を巻き起こしてしまう。

　韓国が日本に対して非常に難しい感情を抱いていること

(注) 2015年12月28日、日韓両政府は慰安婦問題の「最終的かつ不可逆的」解決で合意した。

I know. The historical fact… I don't really understand the old history and its real fact, but as a businessman, the Korean attitude is not so good for business partnership, so they will get worse and worse in economy.

Ms. Park, the president, made a great mistake, I guess. "Japan was a bad country" — all the people of the world thought so 70 years ago, but now, Japan is one of the countries leading the world, so they must have some kind of respectful attitude toward Japan. It's the middle way, I think. But this problem is very difficult.

It's a very difficult matter, so I cannot say decisive things. But if Korean people want to become happier, they should abandon such kind of opinion. They are bad in their attitude. They want to belong to the U.S., China, Japan or North Korea. They are floating now, so they must be serious about their future. They are floating.

Oikawa I'm very surprised. You seem to like Japan.

Trump's G.S. Yeah, of course, of course! I like *geisha*

は、知ってるよ。歴史上の事実は……古い歴史や本当の事実についてはよく知らんけど、ビジネスマンとして言えば、韓国の姿勢はビジネスの相手として、あまり良くないから、経済がどんどん悪くなっていくだろうね。

　朴(パク)大統領は、大きな間違いを犯したと思う。７０年前は世界中の人が「日本は悪い国だ」と思っていたけど、今では日本は世界をリードする国の一つなんだから、日本を尊敬する姿勢みたいなものがないといけない。それが「中道」だと思うね。非常に難しい問題だが。

　この問題は非常に難しいから、あまり断定的なことは言えない。ただ、韓国人がもっと幸せになりたいなら、そういう意見は捨てるべきだろうね。彼らの態度は良くない。アメリカか中国か、日本か、さもなくば北朝鮮の一部になりたがってる。今の韓国はフラフラしてるんで、自分たちの未来について真剣に考えないと駄目だね。フラフラしてるから。

及川　これは驚きました。日本がお好きなようですね。

トランプ守護霊　ああ、当然だよ、当然！　ゲイシャもフ

and *fuji-yama* [audience laugh]. Geisha, fuji-yama and Happy Science. I like… I love them.

Oikawa But in your campaign, you criticized Japan. You attacked Japan over the international trade.

Trump's G.S. Small point, small point. It's a very small point. OK? I love Japan, of course.

If I were Putin, I would do something this year

Oikawa OK. Moving on to the Russian problem. About the Russian president. Since the Ukrainian crisis two years ago, American politicians like Obama, Hillary and everybody else criticized and said, "Putin is the modern Hitler." However, you said Putin is the only effective leader in the world.* Why are you so comfortable praising him?

---

* Trump's statement made in a TV show on December 18, 2015.

ジヤマも好き(会場笑)。ゲイシャ、フジヤマ、幸福の科学。好きで……大好きだねえ。

及川　しかし選挙演説では、日本を批判されていましたよね。国際貿易のことで日本を非難されていました。

トランプ守護霊　小さい、小さい。すごく細かいことじゃないか。もちろん、日本は大好きですよ。

「もし私がプーチンなら、今年、何かをやる」

及川　分かりました。では、ロシア問題に移ります。ロシア大統領についてです。二年前のウクライナ問題以降、オバマやヒラリーなどアメリカの政治家は皆、「プーチンは現代のヒットラーだ」と言って批判しています。しかし、あなたは「プーチンは世界で唯一、力のあるリーダーだ」と言っています(注)。なぜ、そこまで平気でプーチンを称賛されるのでしょうか。

(注) 2015年12月18日のテレビ番組での発言。

Trump's G.S. He has real leadership and he can make decisions. He is a real power holder, I think. In some meaning, I respect him.

It's very difficult to say, but if I were in his place, I would do something this year, 2016, because there is Obama in America. The presidency of Obama is weak. Weakest presidency, so Putin can do everything. Before my presidency, he can do everything. This is a very difficult year for the U.S., but a very convenient year for Russia. He is the world leader now, but next year, I will be the strongest person in the world. So, only this year, you must be careful and be wise.

Oikawa If you really become the U.S. president, will you allow the Japanese government to be friendly with the Russian government?

Trump's G.S. The Japanese government and the Russian government?

5 日米、日韓、ロシア、イラン、中国をどう見るか

トランプ守護霊 彼には本物のリーダーシップがあって、意思決定ができるからね。本物の権力者だと思う。ある意味、尊敬してるよ。

　言いにくいことではあるが、もし私が彼の立場だったら、きっと今年、2016年に何かをやるね。アメリカにいるのはオバマだからね。大統領としてのオバマは、弱いから。一番弱い大統領だから、プーチンは何だってできる。〝私が大統領になる〟前の今なら、何だってできる。今年はアメリカにとって実に難しい年だが、ロシアにとっては実に都合のいい年だ。今はプーチンが世界のリーダーだが、来年は私が世界最強となる。だから君たちも、今年だけは用心して、賢くやれよ。

及川　あなたが本当にアメリカ大統領になられたら、日本政府がロシア政府と親密になることを容認されますか。

トランプ守護霊　日本政府とロシア政府？

Oikawa We have a territorial dispute.

Trump's G.S. Ah, a small dispute. It's a very small one. Please forget about it. If you want your four small islands and want to solve this problem, please buy the Siberian district from Russia. You can. They need money.

China's plan is complicating things in the Middle East

Ishikawa Last year, Western countries and Iran reached a landmark deal on Iran's nuclear problem*.

Trump's G.S. [Sighs.]

Ishikawa And yesterday, Saudi Arabia cut diplomatic ties with Iran. So, what do you think about this kind of…

---

* In July 2015, the UN Security Council endorsed a joint comprehensive agreement on Iran's nuclear program.

及川　我々には、領土問題があるのですが。

トランプ守護霊　ああ、小さいことだ。そんなのは実に小さいことだ。どうか忘れてください。そんな小さい四つの島が欲しいなら、その問題を解決したいなら、ロシアからシベリア地域を買うといいよ。買えるよ。彼らは金が要るんだから。

中東情勢を難しくしている中国の動き

石川　去年、西欧諸国とイランは、イランの核問題について歴史的合意に至りました（注）。

トランプ守護霊　（ため息）

石川　また、昨日サウジアラビアは、イランとの外交関係を断絶しました。これについては、どうお考えで……。

（注）2015年7月、国連安全保障理事会は、イラン核問題の解決に向けた包括的共同行動計画についての合意を承認した。

Trump's G.S. Maybe it's regarding oil price or oil money. Saudi Arabian budget is not so good. Ten trillion yen deficit, they say. I don't know the problem exactly, but maybe Iran and Saudi Arabia would be the next problem. I mean in this area in the Middle East, there is Russia, America, Japan and the Chinese power colliding, so it's very difficult.

The most difficult problem is the Chinese plan. They want to make a new Silk Road. It will be their next target. I mean the starting point of the Third World War.

Ishikawa During the Obama administration, the U.S. is stepping down from the role of policing the world.

Trump's G.S. No, no, no, no, no. Not yet. I'm the next president, so not yet.

5 日米、日韓、ロシア、イラン、中国をどう見るか

トランプ守護霊 たぶん、石油価格やオイルマネーが絡んでるんだろうし、サウジアラビアの財政はあまりよくないからな。10兆円の赤字だって言うし。詳しいことは分からんが、たぶんイランとサウジアラビアが次の火種になるだろう。つまり、この中東では、ロシアとアメリカと日本と中国の力がぶつかっていて、きわめて難しいね。

　いちばん難しいのは中国の計画だ。新たなシルクロードをつくりたがっていて、それを次の目標にしてる。それが次の、第三次世界大戦の始まりになるということさ。

石川 オバマ政権の間に、アメリカは世界の警察官の役割から退いていっています。

トランプ守護霊 いや、違う、違う、違う、違う、まだ違う。私が次期大統領だから、まだ、そんなことはない。

6 What Would Hillary Bring As the President?

Ishikawa I think you said Hillary Clinton was the worst secretary of state in the history of the country[*]. Maybe you need to confront Hillary Clinton, so…

Trump's G.S. Because she is the worst wife of the worst president, Clinton. Why did Mr. Clinton's wife… Hmm… Argh… Bad president! Mr. Clinton was a bad president. And at that time, his adviser was Hillary. It's incredible! She's not a lady! Just an old person! Oh… did I say something wrong? Oh…

Isis I think it's OK.

Trump's G.S. OK, OK. All right, all right.

---

[*] Trump's repeated statement since July 2015.

6　もしヒラリーが大統領になったら？

石川　あなたは、「ヒラリー・クリントンはアメリカ史上最悪の国務長官だ」と言われたと思います（注）。たぶん、ヒラリー・クリントンと対決しないといけませんので……。

トランプ守護霊　あれは、最低の大統領クリントンの、最低の夫人だ。なぜクリントン夫人が……うーん……ああああ……ひどい大統領だよ！　クリントンはひどい大統領だった。当時、ヒラリーが彼のアドバイザーだったんだ。信じ難い！　あれは女性じゃない！　ただの年寄りだ！　ああ……何かまずいことを言ったかな。ああ……。

イシス　大丈夫だと思います。

トランプ守護霊　そうか、そうか。大丈夫、大丈夫。

(注) 2015年7月以降、繰り返している発言。

Isis You said that Obama and Hillary created ISIS and you're going to cut ISIS' head off*. I think this is your biggest thing that you're claiming. How are you going to do that? I just wanted to ask. Do you have any plans?

Trump's G.S. Hmm… Obama has made a lot of deficit for our country, so it's the evil of Democrats. How should I deal with this matter? It's very difficult, but I can predict at this point that if Hillary, Hillary "Clinton" becomes the next president, it'll be the end of the world!

Isis But how do you think the world will end?

Trump's G.S. Because America would not be America at that time. America would be one of the ladies' countries. It would be famous for having a lady

---

* Trump's statement made in his first campaign commercial, aired starting January 4, 2016.

6　もしヒラリーが大統領になったら？

イシス　あなたは、「オバマとヒラリーがＩＳＩＳを作り出した。ＩＳＩＳの首を斬り落としてやる」と言われました（注）。これが、あなたが主張されていることのなかで一番大きいことだと思うのですが、どうやって実行されるのでしょうか。教えてください。何か計画があるのですか。

トランプ守護霊　うーん……。オバマがアメリカに巨額の赤字を作ったから、これは民主党の罪だ。私はこれに、どう取り組むべきか。非常に難しいが、現時点で予言できることがある。もしヒラリーが、ヒラリー・「クリントン」が、また次の大統領になったら、それが「世界の終わり」になる！

イシス　世界がどうやって終わると思われますか。

トランプ守護霊　その時、アメリカがアメリカでなくなるからだ。アメリカは女性の国の一つになってしまう。女性の大統領で知られる国。それだけになる。何の力もない。

（注）2016年1月4日に公開した初めての選挙ＣＭの中での発言。

president. That's all. So, nothing powerful. No ability to consult or to resolve the world's problems. I mean… she is not a decisive person, just a housewife. Oh! [Audience laugh.] Was that a misfire? A misfire? Oh, I don't know.

Oikawa If you run against Hillary Clinton in a general election, according to the current polls, media expect that you would lose badly because of your unpopularity with women. So, how are you going to compete with Hillary? Do you have any hidden cards?

Trump's G.S. Woah… You misunderstood me. [In a low, soft voice] I'm a very sexy person, so I'm very welcomed by women. They are apt to hide their real sympathy for me. I'm a magician that controls women's emotions, you know?

Oikawa Then, are you going to show how much you love women?

世界の問題について相談に乗ったり解決したりする能力などない。つまり……彼女には決断力がない。ただの主婦だろ。おっと！（会場笑）今のはミスショットだったかな？ ミスショットかな？ 分からん。

及川 もしヒラリー・クリントンと本選挙で戦うことになったら、現在の世論調査によると、あなたは女性に不人気なので惨敗するだろうと言われています。ヒラリーと、どう戦いますか。何か秘策があるのですか。

トランプ守護霊 ああ……私を分かってないね。（低くソフトな声で）私はすごくセクシーな男なんだよ。女性には大歓迎されて仕方がない。女性は、本当は私に情が移っているくせに、それを隠したがるんだ。私は女性の気持ちを操(あやつ)るマジシャンなのよ。

及川 では、どれほど女性を愛しているか、見せていくわけですね。

Trump's G.S. I have a lot of experience, so I can. Yes, I can. Yes, we can. Yes, I'll challenge!

Oikawa So, you are sure that you will attract women's votes?

Trump's G.S. [In a sexy voice] OK, OK, OK. No problem. I'm an experienced person, so no problem.

7 Recovering the U.S. Economy

I'm an economist who receives inspiration from Heaven

Ishikawa I think now, the world and America need a strong leader like you.

Trump's G.S. Yeah, yeah, yeah.

Ishikawa Especially, republican voters are frustrated

トランプ守護霊　私は経験豊富だからね。できる、私にはできる、一緒にできる。やってみるさ！

及川　つまり、女性票を持ってこれる確信があるということですか。

トランプ守護霊　（セクシーな囁き声で）はい、はい、はい。問題ない。経験豊富だから、問題ない。

7　アメリカ経済回復のための考え方

天からインスピレーションを受ける「経済の専門家」

石川　今、世界もアメリカも、あなたのような強いリーダーを必要としていると思います。

トランプ守護霊　そう、そう、その通り。

石川　特に共和党の有権者は、既存の政治家たちに失望し

with existing politicians. So, they look for an outsider like you…

Trump's G.S. "Outsider like you"?

Ishikawa Oh, sorry. A new politician, a new leader like you. Actually, some people criticize you saying that you have no achievement, no career as a politician.

But in the business world, you are a real estate tycoon and you have a great achievement in the business world, so maybe you can make use of these skills in the political world. What do you think about these criticisms that say you have no career as a politician?

Trump's G.S. This final year of the Obama presidency, he will make a new bubble [burst]. I will make the U.S. recover from its recession, starting next year.

So, please rely on me. He will make the final disaster for the American people this year. The American bubble, you know? It's a bubble. America's economy is

ています。ですから、あなたのようなアウトサイダーに目を向けて……。

トランプ守護霊　あなたのような「アウトサイダー」？

石川　ああ、失礼しました。新しい政治家、あなたのような新しいリーダーです。実際、あなたには政治家としての業績や職業経験がないと批判する人もいます。
　しかし実業界では、不動産王であり、大きな業績がありますので、そうしたスキルを政治の世界で使うことがおできになるかもしれません。こういった、あなたに政治家の経験がないという批判については、どうお考えですか。

トランプ守護霊　オバマは、大統領任期の最後の年である今年、新たなバブル（崩壊）を起こすだろう。私は来年以降、アメリカをこの不況から回復させてみせる。
　だから、私を信じていただきたい。彼は今年、アメリカ国民にとっての「最後の災難」を引き起こすだろう。アメリカン・バブルだ。分かる？　バブルなんだよ。アメリカ

not good, but he thinks the economy is becoming better and better. But it's an illusion. It's a bubble.

Ishikawa Last year (December 2015), Chairman of FRB, Yellen, raised the interest rate.

Trump's G.S. It's a misunderstanding. It's a mistake in decision. American economy is bad, very bad.

Ishikawa Maybe this year, she will raise the interest rate three times or four times.

Trump's G.S. No, it's a mistake. Our economy is not so good. It's near the next great fall.

Ishikawa So, the unemployment rate is decreasing, but it's not a good decision?

Trump's G.S. I, myself, am an economist and of course a great businessman, so I know everything.

経済は良くないのに、彼は良くなってきていると思ってるが、それは幻想だ。バブルなんだ。

石川　昨年（2015年12月）、ＦＲＢ議長のイエレンが金利を上げました。

トランプ守護霊　あれは誤解だ。判断を間違ってる。アメリカ経済は悪い。非常に悪い。

石川　イエレンは今年、金利を3回か4回、上げるかもしれないと。

トランプ守護霊　良くないね。判断を間違ってる。わが国の経済はそんなに良くない。次なる大不況が近づいている。

石川　失業率は下がっていますが、正しい判断ではないと。

トランプ守護霊　私こそ経済の専門家だからね。当然、大実業家でもあるので、なんでも分かるんだよ。特に経済に

I especially receive some kind of inspiration from Heaven about the economy, so my inspiration is 100 percent correct! Please rely on me.

The new force regarding business

Ishikawa I have one more question on economic policies. Pfizer, one of the biggest drug companies, tried to move its headquarters from the U.S. to Ireland because America's corporate tax rate is very high at about 40 percent, whereas Ireland's corporate tax rate is very low. These kinds of problems occur in America frequently, so Hillary said that America needs to solve these kinds of problems. What do you think about these tax rate issues?

Trump's G.S. Uh-huh. Hmm… [Claps his hands a few times.] Economic growth is first, I think. It comes first. And next is [to resolve] financial deficit, I think. Japan must obey this rule. If Mr. Abe, the Japanese prime

関しては、天からインスピレーションを受けることができるんで、私のインスピレーションは１００パーセント正しい！ 頼りにしてください。

ビジネスのための新たな「フォース」(力)

石川　経済政策についてもう一つ質問があります。ファイザーという最大手の製薬会社が本部をアメリカからアイルランドに移転しようとしています。アメリカの法人税率が約４０％と非常に高いのに対し、アイルランドの法人税率は低いからです。こうした問題がアメリカで頻繁に起きるので、ヒラリーも、こうした問題を解決する必要があると言っていました。こうした税率については、どうお考えですか。

トランプ守護霊　なるほど。 うーん……。(手を数回たたく)「まず経済成長ありき」だと思うね。それが先決だ。財政赤字(の解決)はその次だと思う。日本もこの法則に従うべきだ。日本の首相の安倍さんが、「まず財政赤字あ

minister, chooses the policy of financial deficit first and then economic growth, he will fail in the recovery of the Japanese economy.

Ishikawa So, even in America, you think you need to decrease the corporate tax rate?

Trump's G.S. Hmm… maybe. Maybe. May… be!

Oikawa What about the individual income tax rate?

Trump's G.S. Individual income tax… I hate communism-like equality because wealth is for the people who earn money by themselves and for themselves. I, myself, made a lot of wealth. But it's not unfair, I think. It's just based on my thinking method and my efforts.

You already know that "think big" is a great method. I, myself, experienced that "think big"

りき。次に経済成長」という政策を選択したら、日本経済の回復には失敗するだろう。

石川　では、アメリカも法人税を引き下げるべきだというお考えですか。

トランプ守護霊　うーん……そうかもしれない。そうかも。そう……かも！

及川　個人の所得税については、いかがでしょうか。

トランプ守護霊　個人所得税か……。共産主義的な平等は好きじゃない。富というのは、自分の力で、自分で金を稼いだ人のためのものだからね。私自身、大きな富を手にしたけれども、それはアンフェア（不公平）だとは思わない。自分の考え方や努力に基づくものだからだ。

　「シンク・ビッグ（Think Big＝大きく考える）」が素晴らしい方法であるというのは、君たちもすでにご存じだけ

attitude is the acceleration for personal business grade-up. How to find the balance between "think big" and "be careful" is the crucial point of real management. I did and I could do so. This is my starting point.

In the financial meaning, I'm a great person and a wealthy person. But to become wealthy, personally, we need the attitude of "think big" and at the same time, of "be careful." These two things are very difficult. Very easy to say, but very difficult to carry out. So, these kinds of personal efforts are required for every American businessman and businesswoman. It's the new meaning of the "business force." I think so.

I want to push forward such kind of people who have this new force regarding business. So, it's very difficult to just say, "lower taxes or higher taxes." It's easy to say, but it's difficult. If I make a misleading concept, it will be communitarian-like thinking.

I want to keep on cherishing the American economic

ど、私自身も、「シンク・ビッグ」な態度のおかげで自分のビジネスのグレードアップが加速するという経験をした。「シンク・ビッグ」と「ビー・ケアフル（慎重になる）」——この二つのバランスをいかに取るかが、現実の事業経営における急所なんだ。私はそれをやり、それができた。そこが私の原点だ。

　経済面では、私は大人物で裕福だ。だが個人としては、豊かになるには「シンク・ビッグ」な態度が要ると同時に、「注意深さ」も要る。この二つは実に難しい。言うは易く、実行は実に難しい。だから、こういった個人の努力が、すべてのアメリカ人のビジネスマン、ビジネスウーマンに求められる。それこそが「ビジネス・フォース（力）」の新しい意味だと思う。

　私は、ビジネスに関して新たな「フォース」を持っているような人たちを引き上げたいと思ってるんだよ。だから、単に「減税か増税か」を言うのは難しいね。言うのは簡単だが、難しい。もし考え方を間違えば、共産主義者的な考え方になってしまう。

　私はアメリカ経済の成長力を大切にして、実際にそうい

growth power and those who carry out such kind of attitude. I respect such kind of people and I want to help such kind of people. I'm quite different from communitarian people, so America must destroy Democrats. They are almost equal to communism. I hate such kind of communism.

I believe in God

Ishikawa Yeah. Actually, I think you are a very merciful person.

Trump's G.S. Ah, yeah.

Ishikawa I read your book, written with Robert Kiyosaki, the author of *Rich Dad, Poor Dad*. The title is, *Why We Want You to Be Rich*. In America, middle-class people are very important, so I think you are very merciful and you want to get rid of poverty from this world. Maybe you are influenced by Norman Vincent Peale.

う態度を実践している人たちを守りたい。そういう人は尊敬できるし、助けたいと思う。私は共産主義者とは全く違う。アメリカは民主党を滅ぼすべきだ。彼らは共産主義も同然だ。そういう共産主義は嫌いなんだよ。

「私は神を信じている」

石川　はい。私は実際、あなたは慈悲の心がある方だと思います。

トランプ守護霊　ああ、そうだよ。

石川　私は『金持ち父さん、貧乏父さん』の著者ロバート・キヨサキとあなたの共著を読みました。『あなたに金持ちになってほしい』というタイトルです。アメリカでは、中流階級の人々が非常に大事ですから、あなたは大変、慈悲深い方で、世界から貧困をなくしたいと考えておられると思います。ノーマン・ビンセント・ピールに影響を受けて

Trump's G.S. Ah, yeah.

Ishikawa I think Norman Vincent Peale was your father's friend and pastor. So, you wrote the book, *Think Like a Billionaire.* If possible, could you tell me the key to success?

Trump's G.S. Oh, my basic thinking and the Happy Science thinking are almost the same. I think so. That's

おられるのかもしれませんね。

トランプ守護霊 ああ、そうだね。

石川 ノーマン・ビンセント・ピールは、あなたのお父さんの友達で牧師だったと思います。ですから、あなたは"Think Like a Billionaire"という本を書かれました。もし差し支えなければ、成功の鍵について教えていただけますでしょうか。

トランプ守護霊 まあ、「私の基本的な考え」と「幸福の科学の考え」はほとんど同じだと思う。だから、君たち幸

Norman Vincent Peale [1898~1993] was an American minister and author. A progenitor of "positive thinking." His book, *The Power of Positive Thinking* became a bestseller, selling 20 million copies worldwide. Peale is currently one of the guiding spirits of Happy Science. His spiritual message has been published with the title, *The World of "Positive Thinking"—Spiritual Interview with N. V. Peale*—[photo: published by Happy Science, 2015, English-Japanese bitext].

ノーマン・ビンセント・ピール（1898 - 1993）はアメリカの牧師・著作家。ポジティブ・シンキング（積極思考）の創始者的存在であり、著書『積極的思考の力』は全世界で２千万部の大ベストセラーとなった。現在は幸福の科学の指導霊団の一員であり、英語霊言『「積極思考」の世界―ノーマン・V・ピールの霊言』が発刊されている（写真。2015 年・幸福の科学会内経典。英日対訳）。

why you, Happy Science people, should support me!

I think big, you think big. I think carefully, you think carefully. I think worldwide and you think worldwide. I believe in God and you believe in God. So, we are the same. So, my success is your success. Your success is my success.

Please support me. Any money is welcome or I just want your pure heart for the God of prosperity. I'm the God of prosperity, himself. So, let's be friends. We must be friends.

8 Expectations for the Muslim Immigrants in the U.S.

Isis On one side, you are trying to cut off Muslim people from entering America, but on the other hand, I saw some kind of a speech that you made. You had a Q and A session with high school students in America and one student asked you that there are a lot of

福の科学の人は、私を支持すべきです！

　私は「シンク・ビッグ」で、君たちも「シンク・ビッグ」。私は注意深く考え、君たちも注意深く考える。私は世界規模で考え、君たちも世界規模で考える。そして、私は神を信じているし、君たちも神を信じている。だから、私たちは同じなんだよ。私の成功は君たちの成功で、君たちの成功は私の成功だ。

　ぜひ、私を支持してください。お金は金額にかかわらず有り難いし、あるいは、繁栄の神に捧げる清い心だけでも結構です。私は繁栄の神そのものですから。だから、友人になることだね。われわれは友人にならなければ。

8　米国内のムスリム移民に望むこと

イシス　あなたは一方で、ムスリムの人々をアメリカに入れないようにしようとしています。でも、もう一方では、あなたのスピーチか何かを見たのですが、アメリカの高校生との質疑応答で、ある高校生があなたに質問していました。「アメリカには優秀な国民でムスリムの人がたくさん

talented Muslim Americans in the United States, but are you not going to use their powers? Then, you said that you're going to use them if they have power and you are willing to use them in your cabinet, too. So, I think you have a generous heart... You don't have a problem with that, right?

You have a daughter who married a Jew and is now Jewish. So, I was thinking that maybe you are generous to all religions. Can I ask what kind of belief you have?

Trump's G.S. In business, we have diversity. I mean that we must have friendship for different types of people or different people in belief, so I don't exclude Muslim people in reality.

But in America, there is a feeling about the terrorist attacks. Terrorism is the next great matter, so we must minimize that risk. So, we must be careful of their entering our country in order to protect against a

います。彼らの力を使わないのですか」と。あなたは、「力のある人なら使っていきたいし、自分の閣僚としても使う用意はある」と答えていました。ですから、あなたは心の広い方だと……。その点は構わないということでしょうか。

 あなたのお嬢さんはユダヤ人と結婚されたので、お嬢さんもユダヤ人になられたわけですよね。ですので、あらゆる宗教に対して寛容でいらっしゃるのかなと思っていました。ご自身はどのような信仰をお持ちなのか、お尋ねしたいのですが。

トランプ守護霊 ビジネスは、多様性があるものなんだ。つまり、いろんなタイプの人や、いろんな信仰を持つ人と仲良くしなければいかんから、私は実際、ムスリムを排除(はいじょ)したりはしない。
 だが、アメリカにはテロ攻撃に対する懸念(けねん)がある。テロが次なる大問題なので、そのリスクを最小限に抑えないといけない。だから大惨事を防ぐためには、彼らがアメリカに入って来ることに対して気をつけないといけない。

great disaster.

But in reality, I don't hate Muslim people. If they can change their attitude to become friends and act like Americans, then we can be friends and become business partners. We can, of course, appoint them as, for example, my cabinet people or hire them in my company.

But one point I must point out is that they are very obstinate and they hesitate to change. America is a country of change, so a person who cannot change in the United States is not an American.

America gathered a lot of people from a lot of countries. We welcome them. We used to welcome them, but Muslim people are very negative toward changing their life, their attitude or their thinking pattern; they don't think deeply about their appearances from the outside.

So, if they want to be Americans or people of the United States, behave like that! Then, I will accept.

But if they want to act and say like Islamic people

8　米国内のムスリム移民に望むこと

　でも実際は、別にムスリムが嫌いなわけじゃないよ。彼らが態度を改めて、友好的になり、アメリカ人らしく振る舞ってくれれば、お互い友人やビジネスパートナーとしてやっていけるし、もちろん、たとえば私の閣僚や会社で採用することだってできる。

　ただ、ひとつ指摘しておかなければいけない点として、彼らは非常に頑固だし、自分を変えようとしたがらないところがあるけれども、アメリカは「チェンジ（変化）」の国なんだ。アメリカにいて変化できない人間は、アメリカ国民じゃない。

　アメリカは、いろんな国からいろんな人々が集まってくる。その人たちは歓迎する。かつては歓迎したけれども、ムスリムは、自分たちの生活や振る舞い方やものの考え方を変えることに関して、非常に消極的だし、自分が外からどう見られているのか、深く考えてみようとしないからね。

　だから、彼らがアメリカ人に、米国民になりたいというのなら、それらしく振る舞いなさい！　そうすれば受け入れますよ。
　でも、もし、中東のイスラム教徒のような言動をすると

in the Middle East, it'll be very difficult from now on because there is a crisis for terrorism. To protect this country from terrorism is a very important thing for the next president.

I already warned them about that because I don't want to exclude them, I don't want to kill them and I don't want to give them more burdens. So, before that, I just warned them to be careful and be thinkable; if you want to come to America, be careful and change like an American. American method of thinking, American ways of living and American ways of behavior are required. At that time, we will welcome. Please believe in one sovereign God of the United States.

したら、今後は非常に難しいだろうね。テロの危険があるから。次期大統領にとって、この国をテロから守るのは、きわめて重要なことなんだ。

私がそう警告したのは、彼らを排除したくないし、殺したくもないし、彼らにこれ以上重荷を負わせたくもないからだよ。だからこそ、そうなる前に、「気をつけなさい。よく考えなさい。アメリカに来たかったら、気をつけて、アメリカ人らしく変わりなさい」と警告したんだ。アメリカ的な思考法や、アメリカ的生活様式、アメリカ的行動が求められる。そうであれば、歓迎するよ。アメリカをしろしめす「一なる神」を信じなさい、ということだ。

9 Form a Triangle of God-Believing Countries and Stand Against Atheist China

The successful method for Japan

Oikawa Again, coming back to the U.S. economy, how do you see the U.S. economy recovering, especially this year? We have a common problem, the China issue. The Chinese economy is collapsing now. Yesterday, the Chinese market went down again. So, how do you see this year's U.S. economy?

Trump's G.S. During the Obama period, you cannot expect anything. So, please protect your property. Please protect your Japanese yen and Japanese property.

Please rely on me. If I... no, not *if*, I *must be* the next president. In my presidency, if you, Happy Realization Party? No?

9 「神を信じる」トライアングルで無神論の中国に対抗せよ

日本にとっての「成功の道」とは

及川　もう一度アメリカ経済の話に戻ります。特に今年、アメリカ経済はどのように回復していくとお考えでしょうか。日米は、中国問題という共通の問題を抱えているからです。今、中国経済が崩壊しつつあり、昨日も中国市場が再び暴落しました。今年のアメリカ経済をどうご覧になりますか。

トランプ守護霊　オバマ政権の間は、何も期待できんね。だから、自分の財産を守ってください。日本も、日本の円や国の財産を守ってください。

　私を頼りにしてください。もし私が…いや、「もし」じゃないな、私が次期大統領に決まってるから。私の大統領任期中に、もし君たちの「幸せ実現党」？　じゃなくて、なんだっけ。

Oikawa Happiness Realization Party.

Trump's G.S. Happiness Realization Party. Are you… going to be a ruling party? Is it possible? I don't know. But if your opinion and your activity prevail in this country, we will cooperate, make new leadership in the world and U.S.-Japan treaty will lead the next century. I mean, next one hundred years of prosperity will be promised. So, please believe in me and cooperate with me. That will be your successful method, I think.

Mr. Clinton and his wife used to be your enemies. They made the Chinese economy grow and gave you a lot of sufferings in the economic meaning. They are guilty, so never ever vote for Hillary Clinton. They are enemies of Japanese people. They caused the Japanese poverty, the Japanese economic debacle in the 90s. Hillary will repeat this pattern again, so please choose Donald Trump. This is the fatal point.

9 「神を信じる」トライアングルで無神論の中国に対抗せよ

及川　幸福実現党です。

トランプ守護霊　幸福実現党か。幸福実現党は……与党になるの？　可能性はあるのかな。知らんけど、もし君たちの意見や活動がこの国を席巻(せっけん)したら、我々は協力して、世界の中で新たなリーダーシップを発揮できる。米日条約が来世紀をリードするだろう。つまり、向こう百年間の繁栄が約束されるだろう。だから、私を信じて、協力してください。それが君たちにとって「成功への道」だと思うね。

　クリントン夫妻は、かつて、君たちの敵だったんだよ。彼らが中国経済を成長させて、君たちを経済的に大いに苦しめた。彼らの罪なんだから、ヒラリー・クリントンには決して、決して投票しないように。日本人の敵です。日本が貧しくなったのは、90年代の日本の経済的な崩壊は、彼らのせいです。ヒラリーは、また同じパターンを繰り返すから、ぜひとも、ドナルド・トランプを選んでください。ここが死命(しめい)を制する点です。

Protect against the next Hitler by forming a U.S.-Japan-Germany triangle

Oikawa You are a close ally with Britain. They are very close to China. What do you think about that?

Trump's G.S. They are poor now, so China showed them a lot of money. Our mother country, Great Britain, is sinking now, so it's very sad. Very sad.

But it's OK. Part of my blood is from Germany, so I rely on Germany. German people will change their attitude and mind concept to become the real leader of the EU. Japan will also change their willpower to lead the world. The U.S., Japan and Germany, these three countries will make the next triangle and lead the next economic world.

We must protect against China's hegemony. They are thinking bad things! Spratly Islands, you know? They're making airport in the sea and they want to get the Philippines, Vietnam, Thailand and other

9 「神を信じる」トライアングルで無神論の中国に対抗せよ

米・日・独の三国で「次なるヒットラー」に対する守りを

及川　アメリカと英国は密接な同盟国ですが、英国は中国と深い関係にあります。この点について、どう思われますか。

トランプ守護霊　今のイギリスは金がないから、中国が金をちらつかせたんだ。われらが母なる大英帝国は沈みつつある。実に悲しいね。実に悲しい。

　だが、大丈夫。私にはドイツの血も一部入っていて、ドイツを信頼してるんだ。ドイツ人は姿勢や心構えを改めて、EUの本物のリーダーになるだろう。日本も志を新たにして、世界のリーダーになる。アメリカ、日本、ドイツ、この三国が次のトライアングルを形成し、次の世界経済をリードしていくわけです。

　中国の覇権主義に対して、守りを固めないといけない。奴らは、よからぬことを企んでるからね！　例の南沙諸島だよ。海上に飛行場を造って、フィリピンやベトナムやタイや、その他の国も取ろうとしている。アラビア半島に向

countries. They are just thinking about the new Silk Road to the Arabian Peninsula.

But we must protect against this project because they don't believe in God. We, who believe in God, must gather our powers, control the world, lead the world and make a new world.

Donald Trump is the only one! People who can choose the next president must support me! Rely on me! I will save you! I will support you! I will cooperate with you! I like Ryuho Okawa! I like Oikawa! I like Miss Isis Mariko! And I like you [Ishikawa]! [Audience laugh.]

So, we are friends. Happy Science should dispatch their opinions to all the countries and change the mass media of Japan who are apt to write that Donald Trump is a very dangerous person or that he's a Hitler-like person.

No! The next Hitler is Xi Jinping! That's him! People or a person who can destroy him is the real Christ, Christ-to-be or next to Christ. OK? Don't

けて、「新たなシルクロード」を作るつもりだろう。

　だが、この計画に対して守りを固めないと。彼らは神を信じていないからね。われわれ、神を信じる者たちが力を合わせて、世界をコントロールし、世界を導き、新世界を建設しなければいけない。

　ドナルド・トランプしかいない！　次期大統領を選べる皆さんは、私を支持しなければいけません！　私を信じてください！　私が皆さんを救います！　助けます！　皆さんに協力します！　大川隆法のことは好きです。及川も好きだし、イシス真理子さんも好きです。ついでに君（石川）もだ（会場笑）。

　われわれは友人です。幸福の科学は、すべての国に向けて意見を発信し、日本のマスメディアを変えないといけません。日本のメディアは、ともすれば「ドナルド・トランプは非常に危険な人物だ」とか「ヒットラーのような人間だ」と書いてるから。

　違う！　次なるヒットラーは習近平だ！　あの男だ！　彼を滅ぼす者こそ、真なるキリストである。あるいはキリスト予備軍か、キリストに次ぐ者である。いいですか？　ここ

misunderstand regarding this point.

Ishikawa Then, is joining AIIB [Asia Infrastructure Investment Bank] established by China a wrong choice?

Trump's G.S. Ah, wrong choice. Of course.

Ishikawa How about TPP?

Trump's G.S. TPP, hmm… A little bit of a problem, but Japanese beef is too strong, so this is the problem. It's a problem, a problem, a problem.

But maybe we can make some kind of adjustment. Japanese beef is too high in quality; we, Americans, cannot make such kind of good beef. It's like an American car, so this is the problem. We must persuade our farmers. It's a problem, but we can make some decision.

のところを誤解してはいけません。

石川　では、中国が創設したAIIB（アジアインフラ投資銀行）に参加するという選択は間違いでしょうか。

トランプ守護霊　ああ、間違いに決まってる。

石川　TPPはどうでしょうか。

トランプ守護霊　TPPか。うーん……やや問題だけどね。日本の牛肉は競争力がありすぎるんで、そこが問題だ。問題、問題、問題。
　でも、何か調整できるかもしれない。日本の牛肉は高品質すぎて、われわれアメリカ人には、そこまで良い牛肉はつくれないんだよ。アメ車みたいなもので、この点が問題だね。アメリカの農家を説得しないといけない。一つの問題ではあるけれど、何らかの決定は下せるよ。

10 Trump's Past Lives and a "Big Name"

Isis OK. I'm very honored to listen to your great speech today. Thank you so much.

Lastly, I want to ask you about your past life since you are the guardian spirit of Donald Trump.

Trump's G.S. Of course, of course! You must ask about that!

[Audience laugh.]

Isis Yes, because you referred to God many times.

Trump's G.S. God! Yeah, yeah.

Isis So, can you tell us about that?

１０　過去世を問われて飛び出したビッグ・ネーム

イシス　本日は素晴らしい演説をお聞きすることができて、たいへん光栄です。本当にありがとうございます。
　最後に、あなたはドナルド・トランプ氏の守護霊でいらっしゃいますので、あなたの過去世(かこぜ)についてお伺いしたいと思います。

トランプ守護霊　当然、当然。それを訊(き)いてもらわないとね！

（会場笑）

イシス　はい、何度も「神」という言葉を口にされましたし。

トランプ守護霊　「神」ね！　そう、そう。

イシス　では、お話しいただけますか。

Trump's G.S. [In a teasing manner] George Washington!

Isis Wow…

Trump's G.S. George Washington! George Washington! George Washington! That's me!

Isis Really… For real?

Trump's G.S. For example.

Isis For example [laughs] [audience laugh].

Trump's G.S. [Laughs.] If American people believe in past lives, I must say I was George Washington.

Isis You want to be like George Washington?

トランプ守護霊 (もったいぶって) ジョージ・ワシントン！

イシス まあ……。

トランプ守護霊 ジョージ・ワシントン！ ジョージ・ワシントン！ ジョージ・ワシントン！ それが私です！

イシス 本当ですか。

トランプ守護霊 たとえばね。

イシス 「たとえば」ですか。(笑) (会場笑)

トランプ守護霊 (笑) アメリカ人が過去世というものを信じているとしたら、「ジョージ・ワシントンだった」と言うしかないから。

イシス ジョージ・ワシントンのようになりたいということですか。

Trump's G.S. No. I *was* George Washington. I was. I was.

Isis OK. Are there any others? Do you know Master Ryuho Okawa's past lives?

Trump's G.S. I don't know [laughs]. But he's a great person, I know. I know, I know, I know. He's a great person. I feel some kind of sympathy from him. He might be my old friend.

Oikawa Did you know that he was working in the World Trade Center in the 1980s?

Trump's G.S. Ah... I don't know, but I should know about that. I appreciate that and I can be his friend. We are gods, so gods can be friends [audience laugh].

Oikawa In your soul, do you have any other spiritual

トランプ守護霊 ノー。ジョージ・ワシントンその人だった。そう、そう。

イシス はい。他にはいかがですか。大川隆法総裁の過去世の方をご存じですか。

トランプ守護霊 知らない（笑）。でも、総裁が偉大な方であることは分かってますよ。分かってます、分かってます、分かってます。偉大な方です。総裁とは、どこか、気が合うような感じがする。昔、友人だったのかも。

及川 大川隆法総裁が1980年代に、ワールド・トレード・センターで働いていたことはご存じですか。

トランプ守護霊 ああ……そのことは知らないけど、知ってたらよかったな。それは結構なことだし、総裁とは友だちになれるよ。お互い神様だから、神様同士、友だちになれる（会場笑）。

及川 あなたの魂には、どこか他の国に霊的な記憶があり

memories living in a different country other than the United States?

Trump's G.S. Hmm… In the ancient times, I might have been Jewish. Maybe Jewish. And…

Oikawa Which time? In the time of Christ?

Trump's G.S. Hmm… Hmm… Maybe a famous person, but we are Christians, so it's very difficult to say that because Christian people don't believe in such kind of reincarnation. I have one past life in the Jewish history. Before that, I was born as a king of Egypt. I was a king of Egypt and I made pyramids.

Oikawa Can you reveal the name of the king of Egypt?

Trump's G.S. Hmm… maybe Echnaton [Akhenaten]*

---

* A pharaoh of the 18th dynasty in ancient Egypt, 14th century BC. Known earlier as Amenhotep IV.

ますか。アメリカ以外の。

トランプ守護霊 うーん……古代には、ユダヤ人だったかもしれないな。ユダヤ人かも。それから……。

及川 いつの時代ですか。キリストの時代ですか。

トランプ守護霊 うーん……うーん……。たぶん有名だったけど、われわれはクリスチャンだから、すごく言いにくいんだよ。クリスチャンは、そういう転生輪廻(たぐい)の類は信じてないから。私の過去世の一つはユダヤの歴史の中にある。その前は、「エジプトの王」として生まれたな。エジプトの王で、ピラミッドを造った。

及川 その王の名前は明かしていただけますか。

トランプ守護霊 うーん……たぶん「イクナートン」(注)

(注)紀元前14世紀、古代エジプト第18王朝の王(ファラオ)アメンホテプ4世が、のちに改名して名乗った名前。

or a name like that, I think... You don't believe me, do you?

[Audience laugh.]

Trump's G.S. OK, OK [laughs].

Oikawa Any experience of being a politician in your past lives?

Trump's G.S. I have an experience of being a god.

Oikawa You are a spiritual person.

Trump's G.S. Spiritual person, yeah. King, preacher and a god. At the time of the Crusades, I went from England to Jerusalem and did something. I was one of the generals at that time.

But correctly, I cannot remember. It's very difficult for a Christian person to answer you, so please forgive

というような名前だったと思う。……信じてないだろ？

（会場笑）

トランプ守護霊　まあ、いいか（笑）。

及川　過去世で、政治家だった経験は？

トランプ守護霊　神様だった経験はある。

及川　霊的な方なんですね。

トランプ守護霊　霊的、そうね。国王で宗教家で、神だった。十字軍の時代には、イギリスからエルサレムに渡って、何かをやったな。その時は将軍の一人だった。

　でも、正確には思い出せない。キリスト教徒には、すごく答えにくいので、細かいことは勘弁してもらえるかな。

about the minor details. Please write me in a good way. Your editor is very good at making stories, so I can expect that.

Oikawa He [Ishikawa] is the chief editor.

Trump's G.S. Oh, really? You can make any fiction, then. It's all right. It's an option.

11 Message for the Prosperity of Japan and the U.S.

Ishikawa I have one question. There are a lot of entrepreneurs in America and some of them may want to follow you and become American presidents in the future. So, if you…

Trump's G.S. No chance for them.

Ishikawa No chance for them [laughs]? I'm not sure

何か、いいように書いといてくれ。おたくの編集者は話を作るのが上手いから、期待してるよ。

及川　彼(石川)は編集局長です。

トランプ守護霊　おお、そうなのか。じゃあ、どんなフィクションでも作れるわけね。大丈夫だ。選んでもらえばいい。

11　日米の繁栄に向けたメッセージ

石川　一つ、質問があります。アメリカには多くの企業家がいますが、彼らの中には、あなたに続いて、将来、アメリカ大統領になりたいと考えている人もいますので……。

トランプ守護霊　無理だね。

石川　無理ですか(笑)。マーク・ザッカーバーグが大統

if Mark Zuckerberg wants to be a president, but if you have some advice to young entrepreneurs…

Trump's G.S. They should abandon that thought. I'm the next president. God decides that.

Oikawa This spiritual interview will be published in Japan and also published in the U.S. soon, in English, edited by him. So, do you have any…

Trump's G.S. Oh, it's OK! No problem! He can make any fiction, so it's OK. No problem.

Oikawa OK. Finally, do you have any last message to the Japanese people and to U.S. citizens?

Trump's G.S. Last message?

I like U.S. citizens, of course, I like the Japanese people and I like the Islamic people. In the end, I like all the people of the world.

領になりたいと思っているかどうかは分かりませんが、若き企業家たちにアドバイスをされるとしたら……。

トランプ守護霊　諦(あきら)めるべきだね。私が次期大統領です。神が決めることですから。

及川　この霊言は日本で発刊されますし、アメリカでも近いうちに、彼が編集して英語で発刊されるでしょう。そこで、何か……。

トランプ守護霊　ああ、いいよ！　問題ない！　彼がどんなフィクションでも作ってくれるから、大丈夫だ。問題ない。

及川　はい。最後に、日本人と米国民に向けて、メッセージをお願いします。

トランプ守護霊　ラスト・メッセージね。
　私は当然、米国民が好きだし、日本人もイスラム教徒も好きです。つまり、世界中の人たちのことが好きなわけです。

So, please believe in me. I like Jesus Christ. I love Jesus Christ and Jesus Christ likes Ryuho Okawa, so we are friends.

We have the same aim and the same mission. I am the savior of the United States. If the United States becomes greater and greater, Japan will prosper the next century, I mean, for more than one hundred years. So, please rely on me. We should be friends. OK?

Oikawa Great. Thank you very much.

Isis Thank you so much.

Trump's G.S. You [Oikawa] are a good person. American people will like you. You should appear on TV, on radio or on newspapers in America. No Japanese person can speak English fluently like you. You can. Yes, you can. You can support me. You can. You should take that challenge.

ですから、私を信じてください。私はイエス・キリストが好きです。私はイエス・キリストが大好きで、イエス・キリストは大川隆法が好きだから、われわれは仲間です。

われわれには同じ目的があり、同じ使命があるのです。私は合衆国の救世主です。アメリカがますます偉大になれば、日本も来世紀、つまり、向こう百年以上にわたって繁栄することでしょう。ですから、信頼してください。われわれは仲間になるべきなのです。これでいいかな。

及川　素晴らしいです。ありがとうございました。

イシス　ありがとうございました。

トランプ守護霊　君（及川）はいい人だね。アメリカ人に、気に入られるよ。君はアメリカのテレビやラジオや新聞に出るべきだ。日本人で君みたいに流暢に英語を話せる人はいないよ。できる。うん、君ならできる。私を支援してもらえる。できる。チャレンジするといいよ。

Oikawa Thank you very much, but I have to be very careful about your humor. OK, thank you very much.

Trump's G.S. [Applauses as he laughs.]

After the spiritual interview

Ryuho Okawa OK. He is a nice guy. I think if he were this kind of young person [cover photo of his autobiography], he could have been like John F. Kennedy. He could have gotten more popularity. He missed out on that point, but he's a good man, I think.

America should change from Democrat to Republican. It's time. Then it will help us from China's intrusion. I think so. I can persuade him. Islamic matter is a very difficult one, but we must do something about that, so we'll do our best to make a new age. He's a good person, I guess so.

Thank you. [Claps hands twice.]

及川 ありがとうございます。ただ、あなたのユーモアには、よくよく注意しないといけませんが。それでは、ありがとうございました。

トランプ守護霊 ハハハハ……（笑いながら拍手）。

霊言を終えて

大川隆法 はい。いい人ですね。この（著書の写真）くらい若ければ、ジョン・F・ケネディのようになれたと思います。もっと人気が出たでしょうね。その点は惜しいと思いますが、いい人だと思いますよ。

　アメリカは民主党から共和党に変わるべきです。もう、その時期です。そうなれば、中国の侵略から助けてもらえると思います。彼を説得できると思いますし、イスラム問題は非常に難しい問題ではありますが、何とかしないといけませんので、新時代を拓いていくためにベストを尽くすつもりです。この人は、いい人だと思います。
　ありがとうございました（手を二回叩く）。

『守護霊インタビュー
ドナルド・トランプ アメリカ復活への戦略』
大川隆法著作関連書籍

『バラク・オバマのスピリチュアル・メッセージ』
(幸福実現党刊)
『オバマ大統領の新・守護霊メッセージ』
(幸福の科学出版刊)
『守護霊インタビュー　駐日アメリカ大使キャロライン・ケネディ　日米の新たな架け橋』(同)
『「積極思考」の世界　ノーマン・V・ピールの霊言』
(幸福の科学刊)

『守護霊インタビュー
ドナルド・トランプ アメリカ復活への戦略』

2016年 1月13日 初版第1刷
2016年12月17日 第2刷

著　者　　大　川　隆　法

発行所　　幸福の科学出版株式会社

〒107-0052 東京都港区赤坂2丁目10番14号
TEL(03) 5573-7700
http://www.irhpress.co.jp/

印刷・製本　　株式会社 研文社

落丁・乱丁本はおとりかえいたします
©Ryuho Okawa 2016. Printed in Japan. 検印省略
ISBN 978-4-86395-755-8 C0030
Photo：ZUMA Press/ アフロ /AP/ アフロ
Everett Collection / amanaimages / Scott Olson

大川隆法ベストセラーズ・英語説法&世界の指導者の本心

トランプ新大統領で世界はこう動く

英語説法
日本語訳付き

日本とアメリカの信頼関係は、再び"世界の原動力"となる——。トランプ勝利を2016年1月時点で明言した著者が示す2017年以降の世界の見取り図。

1,500円

Power to the Future
未来に力を

英語説法集
日本語訳付き

予断を許さない日本の国防危機。混迷を極める世界情勢の行方——。ワールド・ティーチャーが英語で語った、この国と世界の進むべき道とは。

1,400円

アメリカ合衆国建国の父 ジョージ・ワシントンの霊言

英語霊言
日本語訳付き

人種差別問題、経済対策、そして対中・対露戦略——。初代大統領が考える、"強いアメリカ"復活の条件。

1,400円

幸福の科学出版

大川隆法ベストセラーズ・世界の指導者の本心

ヒラリー・クリントンの政治外交リーディング
同盟国から見た日本外交の問題点

竹島、尖閣と続発する日本の領土問題……。国防意識なき同盟国をアメリカはどう見ているのか？ クリントン国務長官の本心に迫る！
【幸福実現党刊】

1,400円

ドゥテルテ フィリピン大統領 守護霊メッセージ

英語霊言 日本語訳付き

南シナ海問題を占う上で重要な証言！ 反米親中は本心か──隠された本音とは？ いま話題の暴言大統領、その意外な素顔が明らかに。

1,400円

ヘンリー・キッシンジャー博士 7つの近未来予言

英語霊言 日本語訳付き

米大統領選、北朝鮮の核、米中覇権戦争、イスラム問題、EU危機など、いま世界が抱える7つの問題に対し、国際政治学の権威が大胆に予測！

1,500円

※表示価格は本体価格（税別）です。

大川隆法ベストセラーズ・世界の指導者の本心

オバマ大統領の
新・守護霊メッセージ

英語霊言
日本語訳付き

日中韓問題、TPP交渉、ウクライナ問題、安倍首相への要望……。来日直前のオバマ大統領の本音に迫った、緊急守護霊インタビュー!

1,400円

守護霊インタビュー
駐日アメリカ大使
キャロライン・ケネディ
日米の新たな架け橋

英語霊言
日本語訳付き

先の大戦、歴史問題、JFK暗殺の真相……。親日派とされるケネディ駐日米国大使の守護霊が語る、日本への思いと日米の未来。

1,400円

キング牧師
天国からのメッセージ

アメリカの課題と夢

英語霊言
日本語訳付き

宗教対立とテロ、人種差別、貧困と移民問題、そして米大統領選の行方——。黒人解放運動に生涯を捧げたキング牧師から現代人へのメッセージ。

1,400円

幸福の科学出版

大川隆法ベストセラーズ・世界の指導者の本心

プーチン 日本の政治を叱る
緊急守護霊メッセージ

日本はロシアとの友好を失ってよいのか? 日露首脳会談の翌日、優柔不断な日本の政治を一刀両断する、プーチン大統領守護霊の「本音トーク」。

1,400円

中国と習近平に未来はあるか
反日デモの謎を解く

「反日デモ」も、「反原発・沖縄基地問題」も中国が仕組んだ日本占領への布石だった。緊迫する日中関係の未来を習近平氏守護霊に問う。
【幸福実現党刊】

1,400円

自称〝元首〟の本心に迫る
安倍首相の守護霊霊言

幸福実現党潰しは、アベノミクスの失速隠しと、先の参院選や都知事選への恨みか? 国民が知らない安倍首相の本音を守護霊が包み隠さず語った。

1,400円

※表示価格は本体価格(税別)です。

大川隆法ベストセラーズ・世界の指導者の本心

原爆投下は人類への罪か?
公開霊言 トルーマン＆F・ルーズベルトの新証言

なぜ、終戦間際に、アメリカは日本に2度も原爆を落としたのか?「憲法改正」を語る上で避けては通れない難題に「公開霊言」が挑む。
【幸福実現党刊】

1,400円

北朝鮮・金正恩はなぜ「水爆実験」をしたのか
緊急守護霊インタビュー

核実験直後の2016年1月7日に収録された緊急インタビュー。
「これで、日本人全員が人質になった」。
国会での安保法制反対をあざ笑うかのような強行実験、その本心とは。

1,400円

潘基文（パンキムン）国連事務総長の守護霊インタビュー

「私が考えているのは、韓国の利益だけだ。次は、韓国の大統領になる」──。国連トップ・潘氏守護霊が明かす、その驚くべき本心とは。

英語霊言
日本語訳付き

1,400円

幸福の科学出版

大川隆法ベストセラーズ・世界の指導者の本心

ネルソン・マンデラ ラスト・メッセージ

人種差別と戦い、27年もの投獄に耐え、民族融和の理想を貫いた偉大なる指導者ネルソン・マンデラ。その「復活」のメッセージを全世界の人びとに!

英語霊言 日本語訳付き

1,400円

アサド大統領のスピリチュアル・メッセージ

混迷するシリア問題の真相を探るため、アサド大統領の守護霊霊言に挑む──。恐るべき独裁者の実像が明らかに!

英語霊言 日本語訳付き

1,400円

緊急・守護霊インタビュー 台湾新総統 蔡英文の未来戦略

台湾新総統・蔡英文氏の守護霊が、アジアの平和と安定のために必要な「未来構想」を語る。アメリカが取るべき進路、日本が打つべき一手とは?

1,400円

※表示価格は本体価格(税別)です。

大川隆法「法シリーズ」・最新刊

伝道の法
人生の「真実」に目覚める時

法シリーズ第23作

2,000円

人生の悩みや苦しみは
どうしたら解決できるのか。
世界の争いや憎しみは
どうしたらなくなるのか。
ここに、ほんとうの「答え」がある。

第1章 心の時代を生きる ── 人生を黄金に変える「心の力」
第2章 魅力ある人となるためには ── 批判する人をもファンに変える力
第3章 人類幸福化の原点 ── 宗教心、信仰心は、なぜ大事なのか
第4章 時代を変える奇跡の力 ── 危機の時代を乗り越える「宗教」と「政治」
第5章 慈悲の力に目覚めるためには ── 一人でも多くの人に愛の心を届けたい
第6章 信じられる世界へ ── あなたにも、世界を幸福に変える「光」がある

幸福の科学出版

大川隆法シリーズ・最新刊

経営戦略の転換点
危機を乗りこえる経営者の心得

経営者は、何を「選び」、何を「捨て」、そして何を「見抜く」べきか。"超"乱気流時代を生き抜く経営マインドと戦略ビジョンを示した一冊。

豪華装丁函入り

10,000円

映画「君の名は。」メガヒットの秘密
新海誠監督の
クリエイティブの源泉に迫る

緻密な風景描写と純粋な心情表現が共感を誘う「新海ワールド」──。その世界観、美的感覚、そして監督自身の本心に迫る守護霊インタビュー。

1,400円

守護霊メッセージ
女優・芦川よしみ
演技する心

芸能界で40年以上活躍しつづけるベテラン女優の「プロフェッショナル演技論」。表現者としての「心の練り方」「技術の磨き方」を特別講義。

1,400円

※表示価格は本体価格(税別)です。

幸福の科学グループのご案内

宗教、教育、政治、出版などの活動を通じて、地球的ユートピアの実現を目指しています。

幸福の科学

1986年に立宗。信仰の対象は、地球系霊団の最高大霊、主エル・カンターレ。世界100カ国以上の国々に信者を持ち、全人類救済という尊い使命のもと、信者は、「愛」と「悟り」と「ユートピア建設」の教えの実践、伝道に励んでいます。

（2016年12月現在）

愛

幸福の科学の「愛」とは、与える愛です。これは、仏教の慈悲(じひ)や布施(ふせ)の精神と同じことです。信者は、仏法真理をお伝えすることを通して、多くの方に幸福な人生を送っていただくための活動に励んでいます。

悟り

「悟り」とは、自らが仏の子であることを知るということです。教学(きょうがく)や精神統一によって心を磨き、智慧(ちえ)を得て悩みを解決すると共に、天使・菩薩(ぼさつ)の境地を目指し、より多くの人を救える力を身につけていきます。

ユートピア建設

私たち人間は、地上に理想世界を建設するという尊い使命を持って生まれてきています。社会の悪を押しとどめ、善を推し進めるために、信者はさまざまな活動に積極的に参加しています。

海外支援・災害支援

国内外の世界で貧困や災害、心の病で苦しんでいる人々に対しては、現地メンバーや支援団体と連携して、物心両面にわたり、あらゆる手段で手を差し伸べています。

自殺を減らそうキャンペーン

年間約3万人の自殺者を減らすため、全国各地で街頭キャンペーンを展開しています。

公式サイト **www.withyou-hs.net**

ヘレンの会

ヘレン・ケラーを理想として活動する、ハンディキャップを持つ方とボランティアの会です。視聴覚障害者、肢体不自由な方々に仏法真理を学んでいただくための、さまざまなサポートをしています。

公式サイト **www.helen-hs.net**

INFORMATION

お近くの精舎・支部・拠点など、お問い合わせは、こちらまで!
幸福の科学サービスセンター
TEL. **03-5793-1727** (受付時間 火~金:10~20時/土・日・祝日:10~18時)
幸福の科学公式サイト **happy-science.jp**

幸福の科学グループの教育・人材養成事業

ハッピー・サイエンス・ユニバーシティ
Happy Science University

ハッピー・サイエンス・ユニバーシティとは

ハッピー・サイエンス・ユニバーシティ(HSU)は、大川隆法総裁が設立された「現代の松下村塾」であり、「日本発の本格私学」です。
建学の精神として「幸福の探究と新文明の創造」を掲げ、
チャレンジ精神にあふれ、新時代を切り拓く人材の輩出を目指します。

学部のご案内

人間幸福学部
人間学を学び、新時代を切り拓くリーダーとなる

経営成功学部
企業や国家の繁栄を実現する、起業家精神あふれる人材となる

未来産業学部
新文明の源流を創造するチャレンジャーとなる

未来創造学部 〔2016年4月開設〕
時代を変え、未来を創る主役となる

政治家やジャーナリスト、ライター、俳優・タレントなどのスター、映画監督・脚本家などのクリエーター人材を育てます。※

※キャンパスは東京がメインとなり、2年制の短期特進課程も新設します（4年制の1年次は千葉です）。2017年3月までは、赤坂「ユートピア活動推進館」、2017年4月より東京都江東区（東西線東陽町駅近く）の新校舎「HSU未来創造・東京キャンパス」がキャンパスとなります。

住所 〒299-4325 千葉県長生郡長生村一松丙 4427-1
TEL.0475-32-7770

幸福の科学グループの教育・人材養成事業

教育

学校法人 幸福の科学学園

学校法人 幸福の科学学園は、幸福の科学の教育理念のもとにつくられた教育機関です。人間にとって最も大切な宗教教育の導入を通じて精神性を高めながら、ユートピア建設に貢献する人材輩出を目指しています。

幸福の科学学園

中学校・高等学校（那須本校）
2010年4月開校・栃木県那須郡（男女共学・全寮制）
TEL 0287-75-7777
公式サイト happy-science.ac.jp

関西中学校・高等学校（関西校）
2013年4月開校・滋賀県大津市（男女共学・寮及び通学）
TEL 077-573-7774
公式サイト kansai.happy-science.ac.jp

仏法真理塾「サクセスNo.1」 TEL 03-5750-0747（東京本校）
小・中・高校生が、信仰教育を基礎にしながら、「勉強も『心の修行』」と考えて学んでいます。

不登校児支援スクール「ネバー・マインド」 TEL 03-5750-1741
心の面からのアプローチを重視して、不登校の子供たちを支援しています。
また、障害児支援の「ユー・アー・エンゼル！」運動も行っています。

エンゼルプランV TEL 03-5750-0757
幼少時からの心の教育を大切にして、信仰をベースにした幼児教育を行っています。

シニア・プラン21 TEL 03-6384-0778
希望に満ちた生涯現役人生のために、年齢を問わず、多くの方が学んでいます。

NPO活動支援

学校からのいじめ追放を目指し、さまざまな社会提言をしています。また、各地でのシンポジウムや学校への啓発ポスター掲示等に取り組む一般財団法人「いじめから子供を守ろうネットワーク」を支援しています。

ブログ blog.mamoro.org
公式サイト mamoro.org
相談窓口 TEL.03-5719-2170

幸福の科学グループ事業

政治

幸福実現党

内憂外患(ないゆうがいかん)の国難に立ち向かうべく、2009年5月に幸福実現党を立党しました。創立者である大川隆法党総裁の精神的指導のもと、宗教だけでは解決できない問題に取り組み、幸福を具体化するための力になっています。

幸福実現党 釈量子サイト
shaku-ryoko.net

Twitter
釈量子@shakuryoko
で検索

党の機関紙
「幸福実現NEWS」

幸福実現党 党員募集中

あなたも幸福を実現する政治に参画しませんか。

○ 幸福実現党の理念と綱領、政策に賛同する18歳以上の方なら、どなたでも党員になることができます。
○ 党員の期間は、党費(年額 一般党員5,000円、学生党員2,000円)を入金された日から1年間となります。

党員になると

党員限定の機関紙が送付されます(学生党員の方にはメールにてお送りします)。申込書は、下記、幸福実現党公式サイトでダウンロードできます。

住所 〒107-0052
東京都港区赤坂2-10-8 6階
幸福実現党本部

TEL 03-6441-0754
FAX 03-6441-0764
公式サイト hr-party.jp
若者向け政治サイト truthyouth.jp

幸福の科学グループ事業

出版メディア事業

アー・ユー・ハッピー？
are-you-happy.com

ザ・リバティ
the-liberty.com

幸福の科学出版

大川隆法総裁の仏法真理の書を中心に、ビジネス、自己啓発、小説など、さまざまなジャンルの書籍・雑誌を出版しています。他にも、映画事業、文学・学術発展のための振興事業、テレビ・ラジオ番組の提供など、幸福の科学文化を広げる事業を行っています。

幸福の科学出版
TEL 03-5573-7700
公式サイト irhpress.co.jp

ザ・ファクト
マスコミが報道しない「事実」を世界に伝えるネット・オピニオン番組

Youtubeにて随時好評配信中！

ザ・ファクト　検索

ニュースター・プロダクション

ニュースター・プロダクション（株）は、新時代の"美しさ"を創造する芸能プロダクションです。2016年3月には、映画「天使に"アイム・ファイン"」を公開。2017年初夏には、ニュースター・プロダクション企画の映画「君のまなざし」を公開予定です。

公式サイト
newstarpro.co.jp

ニュースター・プリンセス・オーディション

ニュースター・プロダクションは、2018年公開予定映画のヒロイン人材を求めて、全国規模のオーディションを開催します。あなたも映画のヒロインを目指して、応募してみませんか？

詳しくはこちら　ニュースター・プロダクション　検索

入会のご案内

あなたも、幸福の科学に集い、ほんとうの幸福を見つけてみませんか?

幸福の科学では、大川隆法総裁が説く仏法真理をもとに、
「どうすれば幸福になれるのか、また、
他の人を幸福にできるのか」を学び、実践しています。

入会

大川隆法総裁の教えを信じ、学ぼうとする方なら、どなたでも入会できます。入会された方には、『入会版「正心法語」』が授与されます。(入会の奉納は1,000円目安です)

ネットでも入会できます。詳しくは、下記URLへ。
happy-science.jp/joinus

三帰誓願(さんきせいがん)

仏弟子としてさらに信仰を深めたい方は、仏・法・僧の三宝への帰依を誓う「三帰誓願式」を受けることができます。三帰誓願者には、『仏説・正心法語』『祈願文①』『祈願文②』『エル・カンターレへの祈り』が授与されます。

植福の会(しょくふくのかい)

植福は、ユートピア建設のために、自分の富を差し出す尊い布施の行為です。布施の機会として、毎月1口1,000円からお申込みいただける、「植福の会」がございます。

ご希望の方には、幸福の科学の小冊子(毎月1回)をお送りいたします。詳しくは、下記の電話番号までお問い合わせください。

月刊「幸福の科学」 ザ・伝道

ヤング・ブッダ ヘルメス・エンゼルズ

INFORMATION

幸福の科学サービスセンター
TEL. 03-5793-1727 (受付時間 火〜金:10〜20時／土・日・祝日:10〜18時)
幸福の科学 公式サイト **happy-science.jp**